Christianity has never lacked articulate defenders, but many people today have forgotten their own heritage. Rob Bowman's book offers readers of all backgrounds an easy point of entry to this deep and vibrant literature. I wish every pastor knew at least this much about the faithful thinkers of past generations!

Timothy McGrew
Professor of Philosophy, Western Michigan University
Director, Library of Historical Apologetics

This is a fantastic little book, written by the perfect person to write it. Bowman's new *Faith Thinkers* offers a helpful "Who's Who" of the great Christian apologists of history and is an excellent resource for students of apologetics!

James K. Dew
President, New Orleans Baptist Theological Seminary

Finally—an accessible introduction to many of history's most influential defenders of the Christian faith and their legacy. Always interesting (and often surprising), Robert Bowman's *Faith Thinkers* will give a new generation of readers a greater appreciation for the remarkable men who laid the groundwork for today's apologetics renaissance. Highly recommended.

Paul Carden
Executive Director, The Centers for Apologetics Research (CFAR)

Faith Thinkers

30 Christian Apologists You Should Know

Robert M. Bowman Jr.

President, Faith Thinkers Inc.

DeWard

for your journey

CONTENTS

Part Two: The Twentieth Century

INTRODUCTION

Two Thousand Years of Faith Thinkers

Christian apologetics is the reasonable defense of the faith, the practice of giving others "a reason for the hope" that we have as believers in Jesus Christ (1 Pet 3.15). An *apologist*—someone who does apologetics—is a faith thinker: someone who thinks about what they believe and why they believe it and then shares their thinking with others. Many Christians are passionately interested today in learning about apologetics. They want to be faith thinkers. Yet the subject can seem intimidating. There are so many apologists, so many books, so many terms that get thrown around, and so many arguments or approaches to the defense of Christianity. It can be difficult to get one's bearings.

This little book will introduce you to 30 books on apologetics issues written by 30 of the most influential Christian thinkers of the past two thousand years. Each chapter provides a glimpse of the world in which these thinkers wrote, especially the challenges to the Christian faith that they faced in their time. Although most of these authors wrote more than one book, in each chapter we focus primarily on one particularly famous and influential book. We look at 15 apologists from before the twentieth century and then 15 apologists whose books appeared in the twentieth century (including a few who are still alive). This means, of course, that books first published in the twenty-first century are not included here. It also means that no women are included among the 30, simply because until recently few women were writing notable books in Christian apologetics. Thankfully, that has begun to change as such apologists as Nancy Pearcey have made outstanding contributions to apologetic literature.

At the end of each chapter are recommendations for further study of that chapter's thinker, both by him and about him. These selections are in many cases very selective, since some of these authors were truly prolific and a great deal has been written about them. The recommendations are usually (not always) introductory in nature and may include some podcasts, videos, or other online resources. I have often refrained from giving the full URL for a webpage since these tend to change every so often, but enough information is given so you can find them using a search engine.

In keeping with the introductory purpose of this book, I have focused on describing the apologists' views with very little in the way of criticisms. Before we criticize the views of others, it is important to have a basic appreciation of the issues and some understanding of the different approaches that thinkers have taken to those issues. Every Christian can learn a lot from all thirty of the authors surveyed here, even those with whom we may strongly disagree on certain points. Becoming acquainted with many of the greatest Christian thinkers of the past two thousand years can help us all to develop into better faith thinkers ourselves.

Many, though not all, of the thinkers profiled in this book were discussed, usually in far greater detail, in an earlier academic textbook that I co-authored with Kenneth D. Boa entitled *Faith Has Its Reasons: Integrative Approaches to Defending the Christian Faith.* (See "Further Resources" at the end for more information.) If *Faith Thinkers* whets your appetite for studying the great Christian apologists in church history, I hope you will take a look at that book.

Part One

Before the Twentieth Century

1

LUKE

Acts of the Apostles (c. AD 61)

> The times of ignorance God overlooked, but now he commands all people everywhere to repent, because he has fixed a day on which he will judge the world in righteousness by a man whom he has appointed; and of this he has given assurance to all by raising him from the dead. —Acts 17.30–31 ESV

Many of the books of the New Testament have an apologetic aspect. However, the two-part history by Luke (his Gospel and the Acts of the Apostles) is the most overtly apologetical work in the New Testament, and it has had enormous influence on apologetics throughout church history. For these reasons, we start with Acts as the first of our 30 books by Christian apologists you should know.

Luke was a physician by profession and a co-worker with Paul in Christian ministry (Col 4.14; 2 Tim 4.11; Phlm 24). He was a traveling companion of Paul during some of his missionary travels and on his journey to Rome (Acts 16.10–17; 20.5–21.18; 27.1–28.16). Acts refers by name to many of Paul's other traveling companions known from his epistles but not to Luke, as one would expect if he were the author. For these and other reasons, the traditional identification of Luke as the author of Acts is very probably correct.

In the prologue to his Gospel (Luke 1.1–4), Luke announced that his work was based on careful historical research and would present an accurate record of the origins of Christianity. It turns out that this was no idle claim. The evidence for the historical accuracy of Luke's work is especially abundant for Acts. Internal evidence, external confirmation of numerous details from archaeology and contemporary literature, and comparisons with Paul's epistles demonstrate that Acts is an impressive work of historical writing in the best tradition of ancient Greco-Roman historiography.

The structure and content of Acts suggests it was written at least in part as a political apology for Paul. Acts ends with Paul under house arrest yet preaching freely in Rome, and it emphasizes (as does the Gospel also) that Jesus and the apostles (especially Paul) were law-abiding persons. The motif of Jesus' resurrection as vindication, his fulfillment of Old Testament messianic prophecies, and the charismatic phenomena on and after the Day of Pentecost are used as cumulative evidences of the messianic lordship of Jesus (Acts 2.36) and of the authority of the apostolic truth claims. Along the way Luke used the speeches of the apostles to present apologetic arguments to a wide variety of audiences, both Jewish and Gentile.

One of these speeches, Paul's address to the Athenians, has been extraordinarily important in Christian reflections about apologetics throughout church history. It is the only substantial example of an apology directed to a non-Jewish audience in the New Testament (though

see Acts 14.15–17). Thus, this one speech has tradition-
ally been regarded as a paradigm or model of apologetics. In this speech, Paul argued in a manner that would
connect especially with Stoics, though his content was
rooted in the teachings of Scripture. He showed that paganism had failed to produce knowledge of the true God
and explained that God had acted to reveal himself to all
people (Acts 17.16–34).

If our Christian apologetics is to be faithful to Scripture, we must pay special attention to the examples provided in Acts.

By Luke

The Gospel of Luke and the Acts of the Apostles are, of course,
found in every edition of the New Testament. Two of the many
excellent study Bibles with helpful notes on these books are *The
Apologetics Study Bible* (Nashville: Holman Bible, 2007) and *The
ESV Study Bible* (Wheaton, IL: Crossway, 2008). *The ESV Study
Bible* can be read free online (www.esv.org).

About Luke

Copan, Paul, and Kenneth D. Litwak. *The Gospel in the Market-
place of Ideas: Paul's Mars Hill Experience for Our Pluralistic
World*. Downers Grove, IL: IVP Academic, 2014. Excellent
analysis of Paul's speech in Athens (Acts 17.16–34).

Howard, Jeremy Royal, gen. ed. *The Holman Apologetics Commentary on the Bible: The Gospels and Acts*. Nashville: Holman
Reference, 2013. A commentary focused on defending the
Gospels and Acts. Darrell L. Bock, the author of the commentary on Luke and Acts, is a leading scholar on Luke.

Keener, Craig S. *Acts: An Exegetical Commentary*. 4 vols. Grand Rapids: Baker Academic, 2012–2015. A massive study that will be a standard reference for years to come.

Mauck, John W. *Paul on Trial: The Book of Acts as a Defense of Christianity*. Nashville: Thomas Nelson—Nelson Reference, 2001. Argues, persuasively in my view, that Acts was written as a defense of Paul's message for the benefit of Roman governmental figures.

2

JUSTIN MARTYR
First Apology (c. 155)

> In order that we may follow those things which please Him,
> choosing them by means of the rational faculties He has Him-
> self endowed us with, He both persuades us and leads us to
> faith. —Justin Martyr, *First Apology* 10.

The apologists of the second century modeled their arguments after contemporary philosophical refutations
of polytheism and the critiques of pagan philosophy by
Hellenistic Jews. Of the many apologists from this period, the most important by far was Justin Martyr (c.
100–165), a convert to Christianity from Platonism. Justin wrote three important works of apologetics, but perhaps the most notable is his *First Apology*. In this book,
addressed to the Roman emperor Antoninus Pius, he ap-
pealed for the civil toleration of Christianity and argued
that it was in fact the true philosophy. About ten years after writing the book, during the reign of Antoninus's suc-
cessor Marcus Aurelius, Justin and six other Christians
were beheaded in Rome for refusing to perform sacrifices
to the Roman gods.

Justin began his defense of Christianity by arguing
that Christians were not atheists. They rejected false gods

and idolatry, but they worshiped the true God, his Son (the Logos, who had become a man, Jesus Christ), and the Spirit. Christ taught a noble, ethical way of life, including obedience to Caesar as long as it did not compromise their exclusive religious devotion to God.

Justin drew some analogies between Christian beliefs and elements of pagan religion while insisting that pagan religion was the creation of demons. Christ was not a magician but was in truth the Son of God. The Hebrew prophets had predicted his birth, miraculous ministry, rejection, crucifixion, resurrection, and heavenly rule. (Justin was a pioneer of the argument from fulfilled prophecy, which he also advanced in more detail in his *Dialogue with Trypho the Jew*.) According to Justin, any truth or semblance of truth in pagan mythology or in Plato's philosophy derived from Moses, whose writings predated them all. (Moses did predate Plato by centuries, but the idea that Plato was in any way dependent on Moses is now universally rejected.)

Justin finishes with a description of the sacraments of baptism and the Eucharist, explaining their origins and refuting the scandalous claim that in the Eucharist believers were literally eating human flesh and drinking human blood. His conclusion includes, ironically, a supposed letter (commonly regarded as spurious) from Marcus Aurelius pleading for tolerance of the Christians.

It is easy for modern readers to find fault with various aspects of Justin's apologetic. However, his efforts were commendable given his place in Christian history (even before the process of collecting the New Testament canon was completed) and in view of his role as a pioneer in Christian theologizing and apologetics.

By Justin Martyr

Justin wrote several apologetics books, three of which are especially famous: *First Apology*, *Second Apology*, and *Dialogue with Trypho the Jew*. The most accessible English translation of these works is still Alexander Roberts and James Donaldson, *The Ante-Nicene Fathers: Translations of the Writings of the Fathers Down to A.D. 325*, rev. A. Cleveland Cox, 10 vols. (Grand Rapids: Eerdmans, 1969 reprint [1888]), volume 1. The text of *The Ante-Nicene Fathers* is available free online.

About Justin Martyr

Chadwick, Henry. "Justin Martyr's Defence of Christianity." *Bulletin of the John Rylands Library* 47 (1965): 275–97. A classic article on Justin's apologetic by a respected church historian (currently available free online).

Geivett, R. Douglas. "Justin Martyr: The First Great Apologist of the Christian Church." The Good Book Blog (Biola University), June 10, 2015. Excellent overview by an evangelical Christian philosopher and apologist.

See also "Justin Martyr (c. 100–c. 165)," at www.earlychurch.org.uk, for a good bibliography of resources, many with links to articles available online.

3

ORIGEN

Against Celsus (248)

This book has been composed not for those who are thorough believers, but for such as are either wholly unacquainted with the Christian faith, or for those who, as the apostle terms them, are weak in the faith. —Origen, *Against Celsus*, Preface.

By far the most important Greek apologist of the third century was Origen (c. 185–254), whose lengthy *Contra Celsum* ("Against Celsus") was a reply to Celsus's philosophical, ethical, and historical criticisms of Christianity. Celsus was a pagan philosopher whose book *The True Word* was written around AD 170. Celsus's book has not itself survived, but much of it is preserved within Origen's book, which contains generous quotations from it. Celsus drew on an earlier critique of Christianity by an unknown Jewish author, and quotations from this "Jew of Celsus," as Origen calls him, are also preserved in *Contra Celsum*. Just as Luke had written his two-volume work (Luke–Acts) for a patron named Theophilus, Origen wrote his work for a Christian patron named Ambrose (or Ambrosius).

In his preface, Origen explains that he intended his work not for mature believers, whom he assumed would not be shaken in their faith by arguments such as Celsus's, but for those unfamiliar with the Christian faith or for new and weak believers. Whereas the second-century apologists had pleaded for imperial toleration of Christianity, Origen pleaded for intellectual respect for Christianity.

Origen's book is difficult to summarize because to a great extent it is a point by point rebuttal to Celsus. It is divided into eight "books," each of which consists of 65 to 99 "chapters" (essentially somewhat long paragraphs). We may identify three kinds of responses that Origen makes to Celsus's criticisms.

First, Origen often pointed out that what Celsus said about Christianity was simply not factually correct or was based on a strained interpretation of the facts. For example, Origen argued that Jesus did not do his miracles by sorcery, and he offered an impressive historical defense of Jesus' resurrection against an early hallucination theory and other objections. Second, Origen turned around many of Celsus's criticisms, showing that what Celsus thought was bad or irrational was good and reasonable. For example, Celsus had faulted Christians for not worshiping the divinity in the Roman emperor, to which Origen replied that either the emperor's divinity was really a demon or it simply did not exist. Third, Origen argued that some of Celsus's objections were based on a naïve, literalistic reading of the Bible. Like many other Christian intellectuals in the early church, Origen argued that some biblical stories (specifically in the Old Testament) were meant to be interpreted allegorically.

Origen's *Contra Celsum* stood as the most successful and valued work of Christian apologetics for well over two centuries. It is with good reason that Origen's book has been ranked as one of the classics of apologetics.

By Origen

Against Celsus (*Contra Celsum*) and other works by Origen are available in volume 4 of *The Ante-Nicene Fathers*, the ten-volume series cited in the chapter on Justin Martyr. See also *Origen: Contra Celsum*, trans. Henry Chadwick, corrected reprint (Cambridge: Cambridge University Press, 1980.

About Origen

Patrick, John. *The Apology of Origen in Reply to Celsus: A Chapter in the History of Apologetics*. Edinburgh: William Blackwood, 1892. Older study that is still worth consulting, available free at archive.org.

Trigg, Joseph Wilson. *Origen: The Bible and Philosophy in the Third Century*. Atlanta: John Knox, 1983. Still standard academic study.

See also "Origen of Alexandria (c. 185–c. 254)," at www.early-church.org.uk, for a good bibliography of resources, many with links to articles available online.

AUGUSTINE

The City of God (c. 413–426)

> But if they do not believe that these miracles were wrought
> by Christ's apostles to gain credence to their preaching of His
> resurrection and ascension, this one grand miracle suffices for
> us, that the whole world has believed without any miracles. —
> Augustine, *City of God* 22.5.

In the early fifth century, pagan religions were on the wane
yet still very much alive, while Christianity was on the as-
cendancy throughout the Roman empire. Then in 410, the
Visigoths sacked Rome, an event that grieved both pagans
and Christians throughout the empire and that provoked
recriminations from pagans who blamed Christianity for
Rome's demise. A response to this complaint came from
the greatest apologist and theologian of this period and
indeed of the first millennium of Christian history after
the New Testament, Aurelius Augustine (354–430), the
bishop of Hippo. Augustine was won to the Christian
faith after trying Manicheism and Platonism, a story he
brilliantly presents in his book *Confessions* (400). While
his worldview was at first heavily Platonic, as he matured
his theology and philosophy became significantly less
Platonic and more and more biblical.

Augustine was the first Christian thinker to set forth explicitly the idea of "faith seeking understanding." In his view, reason helps us recognize that the gospel is true, but we cannot expect to understand everything about it before we put faith in Christ. Instead, once it becomes clear that Christianity is true, we should accept it. Then, from a perspective of faith, we can grow in our understanding. This principle of faith seeking understanding is crucial in Christian apologetics. The Christian faith is reasonable, and we should defend it as such, while at the same time pointing out to people that they cannot expect to understand everything in Christianity before becoming believers.

Augustine's Christian philosophy was developed most fully in one of his last works, *The City of God*. Its 22 books are organized into two main parts. In Part One (books 1–10), Augustine critiqued pagan religion and philosophy, while in Part Two (books 11–22), Augustine expounded and defended the Christian worldview via a comprehensive review of history from creation to consummation based on the Bible.

In Books 1–5 Augustine argued that the pagan gods had proved immoral, inept, and impotent to help their worshippers in this world, particularly in the fall of Rome. Nor was the fall of Rome the result of Fate (Book 5). In Books 6–10 he argued that the pagan gods were also unable to provide blessings in the world to come. Augustine showed that no pagan theology, even the sophisticated Platonist variety, could give true knowledge of God or bring people into a saving relationship with God.

In Books 11–22, Augustine contrasted the "Earthly City" with the "City of God," representing two kinds of people in age-long conflict that will end with the final glorification of God's people. The metaphor of two cities is dependent on the Book of Revelation, in which the city of Babylon the Great (which in Revelation is typified by Rome) falls under divine judgment while the city of the New Jerusalem comes down from heaven.

Augustine's book *The City of God* is rightly regarded as one of the five or ten most important books in the history of Western thought.

By Augustine

Most of Augustine's works are accessible in English in *A Select Library of Nicene and Post-Nicene Fathers of the Christian Church*, 1st series (Grand Rapids: Eerdmans, reprint), available free online. Three of his most important works are conveniently available in one volume found in almost every public library: Augustine, *The Confessions; The City of God; On Christian Doctrine*, Great Books of the Western World, vol. 18 (Chicago: Encyclopaedia Britannica, 1952). There are many other editions of *The Confessions* and *The City of God*.

About Augustine

Chang, Curtis. *Engaging Unbelief: A Captivating Strategy from Augustine & Aquinas.* Downers Grove, IL: InterVarsity Press, 2000. Chang argues that Augustine and Aquinas employed similar apologetic strategies to face very different challenges in their times.

Nash, Ronald H. *The Light of the Mind: St. Augustine's Theory of Knowledge*. Lexington: University Press of Kentucky, 1969. One of the best studies of Augustine, by an evangelical philosopher.

See also "Augustine (354–430)," at www.earlychurch.org.uk, for a good (and quite lengthy) bibliography of resources, many with links to articles available online.

5

ANSELM OF CANTERBURY
Proslogion (1078)

For I do not seek to understand in order to believe but I believe
in order to understand. —Anselm, *Proslogion* 1.

By the seventh century, Christianity had absorbed Greco-Roman culture and triumphed in its struggle against
paganism. The church was the central vehicle of Western
culture, and its apologists during the Middle Ages directed their efforts toward persuading unconverted Jews,
answering Islam, and explicating the rational ground for
belief.

During these centuries, Anselm (1033–1109), the
bishop of Canterbury, emerged as one of the most creative
and original philosophers the Christian church has ever
produced. In his classic book *Proslogion* ("Address"), he
emphasized the side of Augustine's view of faith and reason that viewed faith as prior to reason or understanding.
"For I do not seek to understand in order to believe but
I believe in order to understand" (*Proslogion* 1). Although
his philosophical arguments are often treated simply as
rationalistic proofs designed to convince atheists, for him
they were expressions of the search for understanding of

one who already believed. On the other hand, he did intend at least some of his arguments as proofs to answer unbelievers and to confront them with the truth.

The most famous by far of these philosophical arguments has come to be known as the ontological argument. The essence of the argument is that the notion of a being of unsurpassable greatness is logically inescapable. From the *idea* of "that than which nothing greater can be thought," Anselm inferred the existence or *being* (Greek *ontos*, hence "ontological" argument) of God.

There are many forms of the ontological argument. Perhaps one of the simplest forms (if any of them may be called simple) runs as follows.

> 1. The existence of a necessary Being must be either (a) a necessary existence, (b) an impossible existence, or (c) a possible but not necessary existence.
>
> 2. But the existence of a necessary Being is not an impossible existence because (so far as we can see) there is nothing contradictory about this concept.
>
> 3. Nor is the existence of a necessary Being a possible but not necessary existence, since this would be a self-contradictory claim.
>
> 4. Therefore, the existence of a necessary Being is a necessary existence.
>
> 5. Therefore, a necessary Being necessarily exists.

The ontological argument is usually treated as a rational proof of the existence of God, and as such it has been widely rejected by both Christian and non-Christian philosophers. Some philosophers have taken it to prove that *if* there is a God, he must be a necessary being (that is, a being that *must* exist—that cannot *not* exist) rather than a contingent being (one that might or might not have existed). Others have argued that it proves that necessary existence must be acknowledged for some being, either for the cosmos itself or for a being transcendent to the cosmos.

Anselm's argument has enjoyed something of a revival in recent decades, especially due to the work of Alvin Plantinga, another Christian apologist we will discuss later (chapter 25). However, the ontological argument remains the most controversial and disputed argument for God's existence.

By Anselm

The standard English edition of Anselm's works is *Anselm of Canterbury*, trans. and ed. Jasper Hopkins and Herbert Richardson, 4 vols. (New York: Edwin Mellen Press; London: SCM, 1974–1976). A somewhat more accessible collection may be found in Brian Davies and Gillian R. Evans, eds., *Anselm of Canterbury: The Major Works*, Oxford World's Classics (Oxford and New York: Oxford University Press, 1998). The *Proslogion* is also available free online in older translations.

About Anselm

Bradshaw, David. "Faith and Reason in St. Anselm's *Monologion*." *Philosophia Christi* 4 (2002): 509–17. A Christian philosopher's analysis, arguing that Anselm's other famous work, the *Monologion*, was not an exercise in natural theology (seeking to prove God's existence apart from revelation).

Davies, Brian, and Brian Leftow, eds. *The Cambridge Companion to Anselm*. Cambridge Companions to Philosophy. New York: Cambridge University Press, 2004. A standard reference work on all things Anselm.

Geisler, Norman L., and Winfried Corduan. *Philosophy of Religion*. 2nd ed. Grand Rapids: Baker, 1988. See chapter 7, "Ontological Arguments" (123–49), for a helpful analysis of various forms of the argument. The one presented in this chapter is a simplified version of one set forth in detail by Geisler and Corduan.

Plantinga, Alvin, ed. *The Ontological Argument from St. Anselm to Contemporary Philosophers*. Garden City, NY: Doubleday, Anchor Books, 1968. Plantinga (whom we discuss in chapter 25) helped to revive interest in Anselm's most famous argument with this book.

6

THOMAS AQUINAS
Summa Contra Gentiles (1263)

But there are some truths which the natural reason also is able to reach. Such are that God exists, that He is one, and the like. In fact, such truths about God have been proved demonstratively by the philosophers, guided by the light of the natural reason. —Thomas Aquinas, *Summa Contra Gentiles* 1.3.2.

In the thirteenth century, Christian Europe was shaken by the rediscovery and distribution of the philosophical works of Aristotle and the strong impetus given to the Aristotelian worldview by the very capable Spanish-Arab philosopher Averroes. The growing influence of Averroist thought in European universities led to a crisis for Christian thought. Some scholars at the universities were embracing an uncritical Aristotelianism, while others, especially high-ranking church officials, uncritically condemned anything Aristotelian.

Thomas Aquinas (1225–1274) offered a response to this challenge that would change the course of Christian philosophy and apologetics. In his work *Summa Contra Gentiles*, he proposed a mediating approach that made full use of Aristotelian logic and at least some elements of Aristotelian philosophy for Christian thought while avoiding uncritically accepting everything Aristotle said. Against those who followed Aristotle slavishly, Aquinas was careful to note when Aristotle was not in harmony with the Christian faith. Against the Muslim philosophers who used Aristotle to buttress the religion of Islam, notably Averroes and his followers, Aquinas argued that their reasoning was defective and that their philosophy actually was in conflict with Aristotle properly interpreted. The *Summa Contra Gentiles* is Thomas's principal work of apologetics, while his *Summa Theologiae* is his principal work of theology.

The *Summa Contra Gentiles* consists of four books. The first three examine what can be known by reason but is more securely known by revelation: that there is a God, that he created the world, and that he rules the world providentially. The fourth book treats what can be known only by revelation, such as the Trinity, the Incarnation, and salvation.

Aquinas is perhaps best known for his "five ways," five arguments for the existence of God. Yet Aquinas himself did not put great emphasis on the five ways, which take up only a few pages in both *Summas*. God's existence may be inferred from the nature of the world as changing, causative, contingent, graduated, and ordered (the five ways). These proofs (according to Aquinas himself) show that a God exists, though they do not prove everything that we know about God from divine revelation. For Thomas, faith in God ought to be based on his revelation in Scripture, not on the proofs. The proofs were apparently offered not as a refutation of atheism (which was not a serious option in Aquinas's day), but to show the coherence of Christianity with Aristotelian logic.

To describe Thomas Aquinas as a towering intellect in the history of Christian thought is something of an understatement. His influence in the development of Christian apologetics can hardly be overstated.

By Thomas Aquinas

Aquinas, Thomas. *Summa Contra Gentiles*. 4 vols. New York: Doubleday, 1955–1956; Notre Dame, IN: University of Notre Dame Press, 1975.

_____. *Summa Theologica*. 5 vols. New York: Benziger Brothers, 1948.

About Thomas Aquinas

Davies, Brian. *Thomas Aquinas's* Summa Contra Gentiles*: A Guide and Commentary*. New York: Oxford University Press, 2016. Reliable academic reference work by a respected scholar.

Feser, Edward. *Aquinas: A Beginner's Guide*. Oxford: Oneworld, 2009. Perhaps the best academic introduction to Aquinas.

Geisler, Norman L. *Thomas Aquinas: An Evangelical Appraisal*. Grand Rapids: Baker, 1991; reprint, Eugene, OR: Wipf & Stock, 2003. Geisler (whom we discuss in chapter 23) almost single-handedly brought Thomistic philosophy into respect among evangelical apologists.

Marshall, Taylor. *Thomas Aquinas in 50 Pages: A Layman's Quick Guide to Thomism*. Irving, TX: St. John Press, 2013. Very popular (and obviously short) introduction by a philosopher who had evangelical Protestant theological training but later converted to Catholicism.

7

JOHN CALVIN

Institutes of the Christian Religion (1536)

> Just as old or bleary-eyed men and those with weak vision, if
> you thrust before them a most beautiful volume, even if they
> recognize it to be some sort of writing, yet can scarcely con-
> strue two words, but with the aid of spectacles will begin to
> read distinctly; so Scripture, gathering up the otherwise con-
> fused knowledge of God in our minds, having dispersed our
> darkness, clearly shows us the true God. —John Calvin, *Insti-*
> *tutes of the Christian Religion* 1.6.1.

John Calvin (1509–1564), the sixteenth-century Reform-
er, was the author of the *Institutes of the Christian Religion*,
which constituted the first Protestant systematic theology. Book One of the *Institutes* sets forth a view of faith
and knowledge that has been enormously important in
the development of distinctively Reformed approaches to
Christian philosophy and apologetics.

Modern interpreters are sharply divided on the question whether Calvin allowed for any sort of "natural theology" as part of a Christian apologetic. According to Calvin,
God ought to be known from the "sense of divinity" within every human being (1.3.1). In addition, God "revealed
himself and daily discloses himself in the whole work-

manship of the universe" (1.5.1). Unfortunately, human depravity has rendered this internal and external general revelation incapable of creating a true knowledge of God, and humanity has corrupted the knowledge of God from natural revelation into idolatry or other forms of false worship. As a result, Calvin concludes, natural revelation ends up giving fallen human beings just enough awareness of and information about God to render them without excuse for their unbelief. This negative judgment of the effect of natural revelation is the basis for what Alvin Plantinga has called "the Reformed objection to natural theology."

Although Calvin questioned the value of theistic proofs, he did not question their validity. He simply viewed them as of marginal value in producing the kind of assured knowledge of God that is characteristic of faith. For his purposes he preferred simple, concrete forms of the traditional theistic arguments. He offered short, simple proofs of "God's power, goodness, and wisdom" from the power and grandeur evident in nature and from the marvelous design of the human being (1.5.1–3). These proofs are essentially concrete forms of the teleological argument. Calvin also presented a simple cosmological argument, writing that "he from whom all things draw their origin must be eternal and have beginning from himself" (1.5.6). Thus Calvin himself used forms of the traditional theistic arguments.

Calvin allows for two legitimate uses of evidential arguments for the Christian faith. First, he teaches that they can be used to *confirm the truth of Scripture to believers*.

Second, such arguments can have the apologetic purpose of *silencing critics of Scripture*. For the most part this means using evidential arguments to answer objections. He insists that there are many reasons, "neither few nor weak," by which Scripture can be "brilliantly vindicated against the wiles of its disparagers" (1.8.13). These reasons include the candor of the biblical writings, fulfilled biblical prophecies, the preservation of the Jewish race, the wisdom of the apostolic writings in contrast with their humble origins, the testimony of martyrs, and more.

The *Institutes of the Christian Religion* is one of the most important books published in the past five hundred years. No one should criticize Calvin without first reading him.

By Calvin

Calvin, John. *Institutes of the Christian Religion*, ed. John T. McNeill, trans. Ford Lewis Battles. Library of Christian Classics 20–21. 2 vols. Philadelphia: Westminster, 1960. This is the standard academic English edition of Calvin's work, with extensive notes.

About Calvin

Jones, Timothy Paul. "John Calvin and the Problem of Philosophical Apologetics." *Perspectives in Religious Studies* 23 (1996): 387–403. Notable article on Calvin and apologetics by a Southern Baptist philosopher.

McGrath, Alister E. *A Life of John Calvin: A Study in the Shaping of Western Culture*. Oxford: Blackwell, 1990. One of the best biographies of Calvin, by an evangelical theologian.

8

GALILEO GALILEI

Letter to the Grand Duchess Christina (1615)

> I do not feel obliged to believe that the same God who has
> endowed us with senses, reason and intellect has intended us to
> forego their use. —Galileo Galilei, *Letter to the Grand Duchess
> Christina.*

The medieval view that the earth was the unmoving center of the universe, known as *geocentrism*, was inherited
from the ancient Greeks and systematized in the second
century AD by the pagan astronomer Ptolemy. Although
the Ptolemaic system was not actually taught in the Bible,
it was easy for the medieval Christian world to read the
idea into various biblical texts. The Scripture most commonly cited to prove the geocentric position was Joshua
10.13, which states that in answer to Joshua's prayer "the
sun stopped in the middle of the sky, and did not hasten
to go down for about a whole day."

The first book to challenge the geocentric system was
written by Nicholas Copernicus, a Polish church official
and physician. His book *On the Revolution of the Heavenly Spheres* (1543) did not overturn the geocentric system
overnight. What has come to be known as the Coperni-

can revolution was fully set into motion by another astronomer about 70 years after Copernicus's death. Galileo Galilei (1564–1642), an Italian professor of mathematics, in 1609 constructed a telescope and used it to look at the heavenly bodies. Galileo saw, among other things, four moons orbiting Jupiter, proving that not all heavenly bodies were orbiting the earth.

When Galileo published his findings in 1609, the intellectual establishment accused Galileo of false doctrine as well as erroneous science, and they goaded various religious leaders into attacking Galileo. One priest, Caccini, reportedly preached a sermon against Galileo using a slightly twisted version of Acts 1.11, "Ye men of Galileo, why stand ye gazing up into heaven?" The main text, though, used against Galileo was the reference to the sun standing still (Josh 10.13), mentioned earlier.

Galileo responded to these theological criticisms in the *Letter to the Grand Duchess Christina* (1615). Galileo argued in this letter that biblical passages such as Joshua 10.13 spoke in ordinary language and described physical events as they appeared to human observers. That the event in Joshua occurred and was a miracle, Galileo did not doubt; but that the Bible meant to specify precisely how the event occurred, and to teach a particular system of astronomy, Galileo pointedly denied. In his view "the holy Bible and the phenomena of nature proceed alike from the divine Word," so that God is no less "excellently revealed in Nature's actions than in the sacred statements of the Bible." Galileo pleaded eloquently for the freedom to study the facts of nature unhindered by theological interpretations of the Bible. To disallow such inquiry, Galileo warned, "it would be necessary to forbid men to look at the heavens," and would implicitly impugn the many Scriptures which teach that God is revealed "in the open book of heaven." Throughout his life Galileo upheld the complete truth of the Bible and its authority.

The *Letter to the Grand Duchess Christina* is the first great modern work on the relationship between science and theology. It remains worth reading to this day.

By Galileo

Drake, Stillman, trans. *Discoveries and Opinions of Galileo*. Garden City, NY: Doubleday—Anchor, 1957. Includes Galileo's book *The Starry Messenger* and his *Letter to the Grand Duchess Christina*. There are many other English editions of Galileo's works, but this remains the classic.

About Galileo

Block, David L., and Kenneth C. Freeman. *God and Galileo: What a 400-Year-Old Letter Teaches Us about Faith and Science*. Wheaton, IL: Crossway, 2019. Uses Galileo's *Letter to the Grand Duchess Christina* as the springboard for challenging atheistic views of science.

9

HUGO GROTIUS

On the Truth of the Christian Religion (1627)

> I am persuaded, that truth is no other way to be defended but
> by truth, and that such as the mind is fully satisfied with; it
> being in vain to attempt to persuade others to that which you
> yourself are not convinced of. —Hugo Grotius, *On the Truth of
> the Christian Religion* 1.1.

The first widely influential modern book of Christian
apologetics was written by Hugo Grotius (1583–1645),
whose main claim to fame lies in a completely different
field. Grotius (also known as Hugo de Groot) is widely
credited with articulating for the first time a clear theory
of international law, in which nations form legally binding
agreements for the purpose of peace. He was also a significant figure in the development of Arminian theology,
though he was mainly concerned for its tolerance in his
predominantly Calvinist country. Imagine the international legal scholar and Lutheran apologist John Warwick
Montgomery (whom we will discuss in a chapter 22) as an
early modern Dutchman and you will be pretty close to
imagining Hugo Grotius.

One rather unusual feature of Grotius's apologetics book was that he wrote it originally in Dutch verse. Grotius composed the book while he was in prison. Fittingly, he escaped in a book chest. In exile in Paris, Grotius translated the work into Latin prose as *De veritate religionis Christianae*, "On the Truth of the Christian Religion." The book enjoyed great success for the next two centuries, going through 74 editions and 87 translations of either the Dutch or Latin work.

The originality of Grotius's apologetic lay not so much in its content, much of which Grotius had derived from a few earlier sources, but rather in the way this material was put together and the specific purpose for which it was written. Grotius deliberately focused his apology on the truth of Christianity in general, seeking to present a defense of the Christian faith to which Christians of differing—and sometimes violently clashing—theologies could all give assent. In a way, Grotius's *On the Truth of the Christian Religion* was a kind of "Mere Christianity" three centuries before C. S. Lewis.

Grotius's work exhibits the apologetic method commonly called classical apologetics. He first argues that God exists and does miracles (Book I), that Jesus was a real person who presented noble teachings and performed great miracles, including his resurrection from the dead (Book II), and only then defends the authority of the New Testament as Scripture (Book III). The rest of the work offers a refutation of the three main alternative belief systems known in Grotius's civilization: paganism or heathen religion (Book IV), Judaism (Book V), and Islam, known in the West at the time as Mahometanism (Book VI).

On the Truth of the Christian Religion deserves to be remembered as one of the most influential works of Christian apologetics.

By Grotius

Grotius, Hugo. *The Truth of the Christian Religion.* With Jean Le Clerc's Notes and Additions. Trans. John Clarke (1743). Ed. with an introduction by Maria Rosa Antognazza; Knud Haakonssen, gen. ed. Natural Law and Enlightenment Classics. Indianapolis: Liberty Fund, 2012. The 1829 edition of Clarke's translation is available free online: https://www.ccel.org/ccel/grotius.

About Grotius

Heering, Jan Paul. *Hugo Grotius as Apologist for the Christian Religion: A Study of His Work* de Veritate Religionis Christianae *(1640).* Studies in the History of Christian Traditions 111. Leiden: Brill, 2004. Valuable academic study of Grotius's book, tracing its sources and explaining its arguments in his historical context.

"Hugo Grotius." The Thinking Fellows podcast, June 23, 2017. https://www.1517.org/podcasts/the-thinking-fellows/hugo-grotius. Reformation-oriented podcast devotes a whole program to Grotius.

10

BLAISE PASCAL
Pensées (1669)

We must begin by showing that religion is not contrary to reason; that it is venerable, to inspire respect for it; then we must make it lovable, to make good men hope it is true; finally, we must prove it is true. —Blaise Pascal, *Pensées*, no. 187.

One of the most brilliant and original thinkers in human history is the French polymath Blaise Pascal (1623–1662). Despite dying before reaching the age of 40, Pascal made significant contributions to mathematics, physics, technology, literature, theology, and philosophy. Pascal was an early advocate of what was dubbed Jansenism, a Catholic movement that emphasized a staunchly Augustinian understanding of human nature, sin, and salvation that the Catholic hierarchy regarded as uncomfortably close to Calvinism. During his last years, he worked on a book defending the faith that was incomplete when he died. His notes were gathered together and published as *Pensées* ("Thoughts"). To this day there is dispute among scholars regarding the best arrangement of these notes, which are published as a loose collection of numbered sections of varying lengths.

In number 60 Pascal summarized what were evidently to be two major points developed in his work. The first part he entitled "Misery of man without God" or "That nature is corrupt. Proved by nature itself," and the second part "Happiness of man with God" or "That there is a Redeemer. Proved by Scripture." Later he noted that "the Christian faith goes mainly to establish these two facts, the corruption of nature, and redemption by Jesus Christ" (194).

The most famous passage in the *Pensées* is known as Pascal's wager: "Let us weigh the gain and the loss in wagering that God is. Let us estimate these two chances. If you gain, you gain all; if you lose, you lose nothing. Wager then without hesitation that He is" (233). Contemporary philosophers have given the wager argument considerable attention, and there has been much debate about it. In context, Pascal's wager appears to be a recommendation to unbelievers to *try* the Christian faith—to enter into the experience of the faithful as a way to faith. If we refuse to believe and act unless we have certainty, Pascal reminds us, we will "do nothing at all, for nothing is certain" (234).

Pascal regarded attempts "to prove Divinity from the works of nature" in arguments with unbelievers to be counterproductive (242–245). Although he denied that faith rests on proofs, he affirmed that proofs *are* available and offered a brief list of a dozen proofs. These include the establishment of the Christian religion despite its being contrary to human nature; the changed life of a Christian; the biblical miracles in general; the miracles and testimonies of Jesus Christ, the apostles, Moses, and the prophets; the Jewish people; biblical prophecies; and other evidences (289). The rest of the *Pensées* elaborates on these evidences, which provide confirmation of the claims of Jesus Christ in Scripture: "Apart from Jesus Christ, we do not know what is our life, nor our death, nor God, nor ourselves. Thus without the Scripture, which has Jesus Christ alone for its object, we know nothing" (547). The voice of God is clearly heard in Scripture, and for Pascal, the Christ of Scripture is the real proof of Christianity.

350 years after Pascal's death, Christians are still learning from his "thoughts." He was truly one of the most gifted apologists in the history of Christianity.

By Pascal

W. F. Trotter's venerable English translation has been published in at least two important collections: as *Thoughts*, Harvard Classics 48 (New York: P. F. Collier & Son, 1910), 9–317, and as *Pensées*, Great Books of the Western World 33 (Chicago: Encyclopaedia Britannica, 1952), 169–352. There are other translations and editions available.

Kreeft, Peter. *Christianity for Modern Pagans: Pascal's Pensées Edited, Outlined, and Explained*. San Francisco: Ignatius Press, 1993. Catholic philosopher's extremely helpful edition.

About Pascal

Groothuis, Douglas. *On Pascal*. Belmont, CA: Wadsworth, 2002. Excellent introduction by an evangelical Christian apologist.

Rota, Michael. *Taking Pascal's Wager: Faith, Evidence and the Abundant Life*. Downers Grove, IL: IVP Academic, 2016. Excellent defense of Pascal's wager and application of it to contemporary apologetics, endorsed by Groothuis, Chad Meister, and other notable apologists.

11

JOSEPH BUTLER
Analogy of Religion (1736)

Those who believe will here find the scheme of Christianity cleared of objections, and the evidence of it in a peculiar
manner strengthened: those who do not believe, will at least
be shown the absurdity of all attempts to prove Christianity
false.—Joseph Butler, *Analogy of Religion*, 251–52.

In eighteenth-century England, deism posed the main intellectual challenge to Christianity. The deists agreed that
a deity had created the world, but they were skeptical of
miracles and critical of the Bible. Deism flourished in the
soil of seventeenth-century advances in science, especially following the achievements of Isaac Newton, though
Newton was not himself a deist. Of the many responses to deism published in that era, the most popular and
enduring was by the Anglican churchman Joseph Butler
(1692–1752). In 1736 Butler published *The Analogy of Religion, Natural and Revealed, to the Constitution and Course
of Nature*. It was the most important work contributing
to a radical shift in British apologetics away from metaphysical, rationalistic argumentation to a more scientific,
empirical form of reasoning. The long title of Butler's book
provides a helpful summary of his argument. Butler sought

refute the deistic claim that, while natural religion was valid, revealed religion—specifically Christianity—was beset by various intellectual problems and could not be rationally believed. He argued that the problems raised for the Christian religion are analogous to problems in nature.

Butler explained that his argument dealt with *probability*. He admitted that the imperfect character of probabilistic knowledge is irrelevant "to an infinite Intelligence.... But to us, probability is the very guide of life" (2). He then proposed to argue, by probabilistic reasoning, "that he who denies the Scripture to have been from God" because of its apparent difficulties might as well, "for the very same reason, deny the world to have been formed by him" (4).

Butler's book is divided into two major parts, dealing with natural religion and revealed religion respectively. The first division corresponds roughly to arguing for a position common to some forms of deism and Christianity, while the second division presents an argument for what is distinctive to Christianity itself. More specifically, Part I defends belief in divine justice and life after death, while Part II defends belief in divine revelation.

Only in chapter 7 of Part II did Butler offer positive evidences and arguments for Christianity. He argued that biblical history should be presumed accurate in the absence of evidence to the contrary. He pointed out that Paul's epistles offer substantial evidence for the gospel, independent of the other apostles. And he noted that Christianity appears fairly unique in having been founded on the belief in miracles (in contrast especially to Islam, which does not view Muhammad as a miraculous figure). Butler averred that these arguments, taken cumulatively, form a strong argument for the Christian faith. In Butler's conclusion, he emphasized that he had been answering objections, not providing absolute proof.

Butler's *Analogy of Religion* was a landmark work that set the course for the development of what is known today as evidentialist apologetics.

By Butler

Butler, Joseph. *The Analogy of Religion*. Introduction by Ernest C. Mossner. Milestones of Thought. New York: Frederick Ungar, 1961. An older edition may be read free online in several places, such as https://www.ccel.org/ccel/butler/analogy.html, or at archive.org.

About Butler

McGrew, Timothy J. "Lecture 12: Butler's *Analogy of Religion*." Ian Ramsey Centre for Science and Religion: The Deist Controversy series, May 11–July 1, 2015. University of Oxford Podcasts, June 22, 2017. Lecture by Christian philosopher and apologist with PowerPoint. The entire series is worth viewing or listening: http://podcasts.ox.ac.uk/series/ian-ramsey-centre-deist-controversy.

Sanders, Fred. "Butler's Analogy." Scriptorium Daily (blog), May 18, 2009. Short, interesting article by an evangelical theologian illustrating the usefulness of Butler's method.

12

WILLIAM PALEY
Natural Theology (1802)

Were there no example in the world of contrivance, except that of the *eye*, it would be alone sufficient to support the conclusion which we draw from it, as to the necessity of an intelligent Creator. —William Paley, *Natural Theology*, 45.

As deism flourished and contributed in turn to the skepticism of Kant and Hume, apologists increasingly mounted their defense of Christianity on two fronts. On one front they countered the philosophical objections to the traditional cosmological and ontological arguments for God's existence with detailed, empirically based versions of the teleological argument, or the argument from design. This line of argument was sometimes called physico-theology or, more commonly, natural theology. The specific theistic argument of choice became the teleological argument, or more simply the argument from design.

William Paley (1743–1805) presented a classic statement of this theistic argument in his *Natural Theology*. The book begins by introducing and elaborating on Paley's famous analogy of the watch providing evidence of a watchmaker. The bulk of the book consists of a detailed discussion of the arrangement and functions of the various components of the bodies of animals and humans. Evidence from plants, the elements, and astronomy is also adduced. Paley argues that from the "contrivances" evident in nature, one may infer that God is one, personal, intelligent, omnipotent, omniscient, omnipresent, eternal, self-existent, spiritual, and good. In his conclusion he explains the purpose of this line of reasoning. Although he expects that most of his readers already believe in God, he suggests that when that belief is tested, it will be helpful "to find a support in argument for what we had taken upon authority" (278). Furthermore, studying nature in order to find evidence of God enhances our awareness of God's hand in everything around us. Finally Paley urges that the proof of God's existence furnished by natural theology should encourage us to be open to receiving as true whatever revelation God may choose to impart. "The true Theist will be the first to listen to *any* credible communication of divine knowledge." By "credible" Paley means a revelation "which gives reasonable proof of having proceeded from him" (280).

For Paley, then, Christianity must prove itself to be based on an authentic revelation. This leads us to the second front of evidentialist apologetics: its appeal to history. Such proof is to be found, according to Paley and other likeminded apologists, especially in historical evidences for the central biblical events. Paley presented a classic statement of these evidences in his 1794 book, *A View of the Evidences of Christianity*. Yet it was his earlier book, *Natural Theology*, that endured as a classic of Christian apologetics throughout the nineteenth century. The rise of evolutionary theory eventually seemed to blunt the force of Paley's argument—indeed, that seems to have been one of Darwin's principal claims. Nevertheless, the design argument never went away. In fact, it has enjoyed a resurgence in the past thirty years in the light of evidence from the fine-tuning of the universe and the earth and from the information-laden nature of life itself for the existence of an intelligent Designer.

By Paley

Paley, William. *Natural Theology: or, Evidences of the Existence and Attributes of the Deity, Collected from the Appearances of Nature.* 1802; reprint, Houston: St. Thomas Press, 1972.

_____. *Natural Theology.* Ed. with an introduction and notes by Matthew D. Eddy and David Knight. Oxford World's Classics. New York: Oxford University Press, 2006. This is the edition cited in this chapter.

_____. *A View of the Evidences of Christianity.* 2 vols. Cambridge Library Collection. Cambridge: Cambridge University Press, 2009 reprint.

In addition to the above two editions, all of Paley's works can be read free online at archive.org; see the list of links at https://en.wikisource.org/wiki/Author:William_Paley.

About Paley

Geivett, R. Douglas. "Crossing the Heath with William Paley (1743–1805)." The Good Book Blog, June 22, 2015. Evangelical philosopher invites Christians to rediscover Paley.

Wartick, J. W. "William Paley (1743–1805)—Historical Apologist Spotlight." JWWartick.com (blog), June 3, 2013. Nice overview of Paley's life and works.

13

SØREN KIERKEGAARD
Philosophical Fragments (1844)

> As is well known, Christianity is the only historical phenome-
> non that despite the historical—indeed, precisely by means of
> the historical—has wanted to be the single individual's point
> of departure for his eternal consciousness, has wanted to inter-
> est him otherwise than merely historically, has wanted to base
> his happiness on his relation to something historical. —Søren
> Kierkegaard, *Philosophical Fragments*, 109.

Søren Kierkegaard (1813–1855) lived a relatively short
life, during which he was not widely known outside his
native Denmark. Yet in the twentieth century he became
one of the dominant influences in Western philosophy
and theology. Kierkegaard (pronounced *KEER-kuh-gore*)
is generally regarded as the father of both religious and
atheistic existentialism. Like many profound thinkers, Kierkegaard is often cited but rarely understood. Scholars
both sympathetic and critical interpret his thought in rad-
ically different ways.

More so than most theologians or philosophers, Kierkegaard wrote out of the intensity of his own spiritual journey. A year after his mother died, Søren rebelled against his
father and sought his escape in a life of wanton pleasures.
His conduct was so colorful that he became the inspiration

for a character in a novel written by Hans Christian Andersen, Søren's childhood classmate and Denmark's other famous nineteenth-century son. The prodigal son eventually realized the emptiness of that path and returned home to his father, who died soon thereafter (in 1838).

In 1844 and 1846 Kierkegaard wrote *Philosophical Fragments* and the follow-up work *Concluding Unscientific Postscript to "Philosophical Fragments"*. He wrote these books under the pseudonym Johannes Climacus ("Johnny Climax"). Kierkegaard's use of pen names was part of his method of, as he called it, "indirect communication." This method seeks to communicate ideas not by directly asserting or arguing for them, but by speaking in such a way as to provoke people to think about them and embrace the truth "on their own." It is interesting that Hans Christian Andersen is famous for his own method of indirect communication, namely, his popular children's stories.

Kierkegaard's writings were a kind of "apologetic," but an unusual one in that its purpose was not to convert people of other religions to Christianity but to convert nominal Christians to authentic Christian faith. Kierkegaard viewed himself ideally called to this work because he himself struggled to become a Christian. Most 19th-century Danes assumed they were Christians but had accommodated the gospel to something supposedly "plausible" and inoffensive. A "plausible," nonparadoxical, inoffensive Christianity is not, Kierkegaard insisted, the Christianity of the New Testament. Although Kierkegaard opposed traditional apologetics, he offered a kind of "indirect" apologetic in *Philosophical Fragments* for Christianity in keeping with his method of indirect communication. The gospel of God incarnate as Savior and Teacher is not something that anyone would invent and indeed something that unbelievers find offensive; it must therefore have been revealed. Nominal Christians vainly thought they were true Christians merely because they accepted the gospel facts. Kierkegaard saw it as his mission to make it more difficult to become a Christian.

Today, Kierkegaard is often seen as a fideist—someone who maintains that faith cannot be defended rationally. That is true, but his fideism should be understood in its context. To put it bluntly, Kierkagaard was trying to reach superficial Christians, not skeptical atheists.

By Kierkegaard

Kierkegaard, Søren. *Concluding Unscientific Postscript to "Philosophical Fragments,"* vol. 1, *Text*, ed. Howard V. Hong and Edna H. Hong. Princeton: Princeton University Press, 1992. The Hongs produced the definitive edition of Kierkegaard's works in English.

——————. *Philosophical Fragments; Johannes Climacus*, ed. and trans. Howard V. Hong and Edna H. Hong. Princeton: Princeton University Press, 1985.

——————. *The Essential Kierkegaard*, ed. Howard V. Hong and Edna H. Hong. Princeton: Princeton University Press, 2000. An excellent one-volume anthology.

——————. *The Point of View for My Work as an Author*. In *A Kierkegaard Anthology*, ed. Robert Bretall. Princeton: Princ-

eton University Press, 1946. Indispensable source for understanding what Kierkegaard was doing in his books.

About Kierkegaard

Depoe, John. "Rejuvenating Apologetics in the Twenty-first
Century: Taking Hints from Søren Kierkegaard." Waco,
TX, 2002. Evangelical apologist explains why we can learn
something of value for apologetics from Kierkegaard. Cur-
rently online at https://www.sorenkierkegaard.nl/artikelen/
Engels/066.%20Kierkegaard_Apologetics.pdf.

Evans, C. Stephen. *Faith Beyond Reason: A Kierkegaardian Account*. Reason & Religion. Grand Rapids: Eerdmans, 1998.
Christian philosopher argues that Kierkegaard was not an
irrationalist and that fideism (the view that the gospel does
not need defending) can be reasonable.

Geisler, Norman L. "Kierkegaard, Søren." In *Baker Encyclopedia
of Christian Apologetics*, 405–11. Grand Rapids: Baker, 1999.
An especially judicious and even-handed critique of Kierkegaard by a renowned evangelical apologist.

14

SIMON GREENLEAF

The Testimony of the Evangelists (1846)

> We proceed to examine and compare the testimony of the
> Four Evangelists, as witnesses to the life and doctrines of Jesus
> Christ; in order to determine the degree of credit, to which, by
> the rules of evidence applied in human tribunals, they are justly
> entitled.—Simon Greenleaf, *The Testimony of the Evangelists*, 10.

Beginning at least in the early 18th century, with some
anticipation a century earlier, Christian apologists often
used legal reasoning in defense of the faith, especially with
regards to the Gospels, Jesus Christ, and his resurrection.
The most notable early advocate of this method was probably Thomas Sherlock (1729). However, the classic ex-
pression of this approach to apologetics came in a book
by Simon Greenleaf (1783–1853), *An Examination of the
Testimony of the Four Evangelists, by the Rules of Evidence
Administered in Courts of Justice*, first published in 1846
(the same year as Kierkegaard's *Concluding Unscientific
Postscript*). Better known now as simply *The Testimony of
the Evangelists*, portions of Greenleaf's book have been
reprinted numerous times over the past 170-plus years.
Greenleaf was a law professor at Harvard University and
the author of *A Treatise on the Law of Evidence*, a standard

textbook on the subject for many years. In what follows I will be citing the second edition (1847).

The original book Greenleaf published was a massive reference work, the bulk of which was a "Harmony of the Gospels" that included numerous, sometimes lengthy notes in support of the accuracy of the Gospels (49–497). The portions typically reprinted are Greenleaf's opening "An Examination, Etc." (1–48) and concluding material on the trials of Jesus (507–68). Also omitted from the popular reprints, regrettably, is Greenleaf's "Note on the Resurrection" (498–506).

In "Examination," Greenleaf begins by urging that those who wish to discover truth must be ready "to investigate with candor to follow the truth wherever it may lead us" (1). He proposes to bring to the Gospels "the tests to which other evidence is subjected in human tribunals" (2). Here is the first test or rule he presents:

> Every document, apparently ancient, coming from the proper repository or custody, and bearing on its face no evident marks of forgery, the law presumes to be genuine, and devolves on the opposing party the burden of proving it to be otherwise (7).

After some additional preliminaries, Greenleaf examines in turn the four Gospels (10–20). He explains that the issue is not whether there is some possibility of their accounts being false, but whether there is sufficient reason to think they are true (21). As long as there is good evidence for the facts presented in the Gospels, they should be considered proved. One of the strengths of Greenleaf's argument is that he explains clearly why the burden of proof is on the critics of the Gospels. He then argues for the credibility of the Gospels on the basis of five tests, such as their honesty, the number and consistency of their testimonies, and external confirmation (25–45).

Greenleaf's book is a classic work of evidentialist apologetics. Its legal evidences approach has influenced many famous evangelical Christian apologists, such as John Warwick Montgomery and Josh McDowell.

By Greenleaf

Greenleaf, Simon. *An Examination of the Testimony of the Four Evangelists, by the Rules of Evidence Administered in Courts of Justice, with an Account of the Trial of Jesus.* 2nd ed. London: A. Maxwell & Son; Edinburgh: T. & J. Clark, 1847. The unabridged edition of Greenleaf's work, available free online at archive.org. The citations given above were from this edition (using the page numbers shown in the margins).

_____. *The Testimony of the Evangelists: The Gospels Examined by the Rules of Evidence Administered in Courts of Justice.* Grand Rapids: Kregel Classics, 1995. Popular reprint of the 128-page 1874 edition.

_____. *A Treatise on the Law of Evidence.* 3 vols. Boston: Little, Brown, and Company, 1899. Reprint, Clark, NJ: The Lawbook Exchange, Ltd., 2012. Greenleaf's magnum opus on the legal principles that he applied to the Gospels.

About Greenleaf

McGrew, Tim. "Kenny Wyland's Critique of Greenleaf." With additional commentary by W. R. Miller. http://www.tektonics.org/wylandwhine.pdf. Christian philosopher and apologist responds to an atheist's critique of Greenleaf's study of the Gospels.

15

JAMES ORR

The Christian View of God and the World (1897)

The reason why Christianity cannot be waved out of the world at the bidding of sceptics simply is, that the facts are too strong for the attempt. The theories which would explain Christianity away make shipwreck on the facts. —James Orr, *The Christian View of God and the World*, 234.

James Orr (1844–1913) was a Scottish pastor and scholar who eventually became a noted professor of apologetics and theology in Glasgow during the early part of the twentieth century. His books were highly successful and popular defenses of Christian belief among evangelicals in English-speaking countries around the world.

In his classic apologetic book, *The Christian View of God and the World as Centering in the Incarnation*, Orr sought to defend the Christian worldview by appealing to the facts. Orr, who endorsed Butler's argument in *The Analogy of Religion* (90), emphasized that faith in Christ commits the believer to a whole theology and worldview that need to be defended (4).

Orr proposes to defend the Christian worldview by an appeal to history, for it brings "all the issues into court at once. The verdict of history is at once a judgment on the answers which have been given to the theological question; on their agreement with the sum-total of the facts of Christianity; on the methods of exegesis and New Testament criticism by which they have been supported; on their power to maintain themselves against rival views; on how far the existence of Christianity is dependent on them, or bound up with them" (43–44). Note Orr's use of the courtroom metaphor popularized by apologists like Simon Greenleaf; he speaks of bringing "issues into court" and of reaching a "verdict." The imitation of legal argument is typical of the evidentialist approach.

In Orr's view, belief in God and belief in Christ "stand or fall together" (65). "A genuine Theism can never long remain a bare Theism" (76). To be complete and stable, theism, or belief in God, must be held in the context of "the entire Christian view" provided in the biblical revelation (77). This revelation is absolutely necessary, because reason on its own cannot arrive at a Christian worldview. Reason can, however, give "abundant corroboration and verification" to the truth of the Christian revelation. This verification, while perhaps not demonstrative, at least is sufficient to show "that the Christian view of God is not *un*reasonable" (111). Orr is confident that the facts, properly presented, can be used to show that objections to Christianity are without merit. "The reason why Christianity cannot be waved out of the world at the bidding of sceptics simply is, that the facts are too strong for the attempt. The theories which would explain Christianity away make shipwreck on the facts" (234).

Some of Orr's views were out of the mainstream of conservative evangelical belief. He did not hold to biblical inerrancy, and he accepted a form of theistic evolution. In the main, however, Orr was a staunch defender of the Bible and the historic Christian faith. In addition to the book we have highlighted here, Orr wrote significant books in defense of the Virgin Birth and the Resurrection.

By Orr

Orr, James. *The Christian View of God and the World*. Corrected reprint of 3rd ed. Grand Rapids: Eerdmans, 1948; Grand Rapids: Kregel, 1989. Originally published as *The Christian View of God and the World as Centering in the Incarnation*. New York: Scribner, 1897. Also available free online, e.g., at www.ccel.org/ccel/org.

_____. *The Resurrection of Jesus*. London: Hodder & Stoughton, 1909; reprint, Grand Rapids: Zondervan, 1965.

_____. *The Virgin Birth of Christ*. New York: Scribner, 1907.

About Orr

Closson, Don. "Why Worldview?" Probe Ministries, 2007. On the history, importance, and potential pitfalls of worldview thinking, with attention to Orr's role in bringing this concept into evangelical apologetics. Online at https://probe.org/why-worldview/.

Scorgie, Glen G. *A Call for Continuity: The Theological Contribution of James Orr*. Macon, GA: Mercer University Press, 1988. One of the very few academic studies of Orr.

Part Two

The Twentieth Century

16

C. S. LEWIS
Mere Christianity (1944)

A man who was merely a man and said the sort of things Jesus said would not be a great moral teacher. He would either be a lunatic—on a level with the man who says he is a poached egg—or else he would be the Devil of Hell. You must make your choice. Either this man was, and is, the Son of God: or else a madman or something worse. You can shut Him up for a fool, you can spit at Him and kill Him as a demon; or you can fall at His feet and call Him Lord and God. But let us not come with any patronising nonsense about His being a great human teacher. He has not left that open to us. He did not intend to. —C. S. Lewis, *Mere Christianity*, 56.

Clive Staples Lewis (1898–1963), known to his friends as "Jack," was almost without doubt the most popular Christian apologist internationally in the twentieth century. Reportedly over 200 million copies of Lewis's books have been sold, including the beloved seven-volume Chronicles of Narnia, a three-book science fiction series, and many other books in addition to his works of apologetics. No wonder, then, that *Time* magazine labeled him the twentieth century's "most-read apologist for God."

Lewis's best-known apologetic work, *Mere Christianity*, was really a combination of three books (*The Case for Christianity*, *Christian Behaviour*, and *Beyond Personality*).

A 1993 *Christianity Today* poll found it far and away the most influential book in readers' Christian lives, apart from the Bible. In its original form as BBC radio talks during World War II, *Mere Christianity* may actually have contributed in some measure to the Allied victory by encouraging faith and hope among the British people.

We will focus here on *The Case for Christianity*, the first part of *Mere Christianity*. This work is itself divided into two "books." Book I is entitled "Right And Wrong as a Clue to the Meaning of the Universe." Here Lewis presents the moral argument for God. He explains that this argument shows that there is a Power, something or someone behind the moral law but does not prove that the God of Christianity is that Power. This Power, however, must be something like a Mind. Since this Mind expects moral behavior of us and we all too often fail to produce it, what we have found so far is bad news.

The good news is what Christianity has to offer, based on God having revealed himself. This is the subject of Book II, "What Christians Believe." Here Lewis argues that neither pantheism nor dualism can adequately account for evil, which is neither illusory nor a power equal to good. This leaves theism, the belief that God created the world and made humans with the capacity to make choices—a capacity we have misused by doing evil. God's response to evil was to come as a human being, Jesus. Here Lewis presents his most famous argument: that since Jesus claimed to be God, he must either be a very bad man (either consciously evil or completely insane) or actually be God. Since Jesus clearly was not a very bad man, he must really be God. Lewis was quite aware, by the way, that many critics argue that Jesus never made divine claims, an argument he addresses elsewhere. Here Lewis focuses attention on the Gospel accounts of Jesus forgiving sins—something critical scholars would have an especially difficult time dismissing as later legend. As Lewis points out, Jesus was either incredibly arrogant to think he had the authority to forgive someone of every sin he had ever committed, or Jesus really had that authority.

75 years after it was first published, *Mere Christianity* is today constantly one of the bestselling Christian apologetics books on Amazon.

By C. S. Lewis

Lewis, C. S. *The Abolition of Man*. New York: Macmillan, 1947. A classic short book warning that relativistic ethics undermines human dignity. It seems almost prophetic now.

_____. *God in the Dock: Essays on Theology and Ethics*. Edited by Walter Hooper. Grand Rapids: Eerdmans, 1970. Important collection of essays that includes "Evil and God," "Miracles," "Myth Becomes Fact," "The Grand Miracle," "Christian Apologetics," and more.

_____. *Mere Christianity*. Rev. and enlarged ed. New York: Macmillan, 1960.

_____. *Miracles: A Preliminary Study*. 2nd ed. New York: Macmillan, 1960. Arguably Lewis's most ambitious, rigorous apologetic work, thoughtfully revised in light of criticisms he received of the first edition.

_____. *The Problem of Pain*. London: Centenary Press, 1940; New York: Macmillan, 1943; paperback ed., 1962. Lewis's insightful treatment of the problem of evil, still somewhat unusual in its approach.

About C. S. Lewis

Baggett, David, Gary R. Habermas, and Jerry L. Walls, eds. *C. S. Lewis as Philosopher: Truth, Goodness and Beauty*. Foreword by Tom Morris. Downers Grove, IL: IVP Academic, 2008. Essays by Peter Kreeft, Victor Reppert, Baggett, Gregory Bassham, and other scholars, many of whom have published one or more books about Lewis.

Bassham, Gregory, ed. *C. S. Lewis's Christian Apologetics: Pro and Con*. Value Inquiry Books Series 286. Leiden: Brill, 2015. Scholars debate Lewis's argument from desire, argument from reason, moral argument, "trilemma" (so-called) argument, and response to the problem of evil.

Brazier, P. H. *C. S. Lewis: Revelation, Conversion, and Apologetics*. Eugene, OR: Pickwick Publications, 2012. Part of a five-volume series of books on Lewis. This book, by Paul Brazier, puts Lewis's apologetics in biographical, historical, and cultural context, and provides an overview of his apologetically oriented work in chronological order.

Downing, David C. *The Most Reluctant Convert: C. S. Lewis's Journey to Faith*. Downers Grove, IL: InterVarsity, 2002. Insightful, detailed biography of Lewis's early life, with important lessons for Christian apologetics.

Marsden, George M. *C. S. Lewis's* Mere Christianity*: A Biography*. Lives of Great Religious Books. Princeton: Princeton University Press, 2016. Informative and insightful study placing Lewis's most influential nonfiction book in its historical and cultural context.

McGrath, Alister E. *The Intellectual World of C.S. Lewis*. Chichester, England: Wiley-Blackwell, 2014. One of several books about Lewis by this respected English Christian scholar.

Metaxas, Eric, host. *Discussing* Mere Christianity*: Exploring the History, Meaning, and Relevance of C. S. Lewis's Greatest Book*. DVD. Grand Rapids: Zondervan, 2015. 170-minute DVD works through *Mere Christianity* through interviews with McGrath and several other noted Christian scholars. There is also a 120-page study guide by Devin Brown.

Reppert, Victor. *C. S. Lewis's Dangerous Idea: In Defense of the Argument from Reason*. Downers Grove, IL: InterVarsity, 2003. Notable study on one of Lewis's famous arguments for God's existence.

www.cslewis.org. The website of the C. S. Lewis Foundation, which maintains a study center at The Kilns (where Lewis lived) and holds conferences and retreats.

And many, many other great resources!

17

EDWARD JOHN CARNELL

An Introduction to Christian Apologetics (1948)

> Bring on your revelations! Let them make peace with the law
> of contradiction and the facts of history, and they will deserve
> a rational man's assent. A careful examination of the Bible re-
> veals that it passes these stringent examinations *summa cum
> laude*. —Edward John Carnell, *An Introduction to Christian
> Apologetics*, 178.

In the 1930s and 1940s, Calvinist philosophers on both
sides of the Atlantic developed distinctively Reformed
approaches to philosophy and apologetics. At the Free
University in Amsterdam, Herman Dooyeweerd published works seeking to show that theoretical thought was
always rooted in a set of religious presuppositions. At the
newly formed Westminster Theological Seminary in Philadelphia, Cornelius Van Til taught his students (through
course notes unpublished at the time) a new approach to
apologetics in which the truth of Christianity was to be
set forth as the only adequate basis for knowledge, reason,
and fact. Gordon H. Clark, first at Wheaton College and
then at Butler University, developed a dogmatic approach
to apologetics in which the truth of the Bible functioned

as the "axiom" of the Christian's belief system. These "pre-suppositional" approaches to epistemology and apologetics posed direct challenges to classical philosophical arguments for God's existence and to modern evidentialist defenses of Christianity. We will highlight Van Til's and Clark's contributions later (chapters 18 and 20).

Van Til had taught a generation of students when one of them, Edward John Carnell (1919–1967), published a textbook on apologetics advocating an approach that integrated Van Til's presuppositional method with other perspectives. The book, *An Introduction to Christian Apologetics*, was published in 1948, the same year Carnell became a professor at Fuller Theological Seminary in Pasadena, California. Carnell evidently suffered from clinical depression, and in 1967 he died from an overdose of sleeping pills. His emotional turmoil perhaps made him identify more sympathetically with Kierkegaard, and in fact he was one of the first American evangelicals to write a book about Kierkegaard's thought. With the passing of time Carnell came to place increasing emphasis and priority on the experiential and ethical dimensions of faith. However, his apologetic method remained essentially unchanged from what he set forth in his *Introduction*.

Carnell held a mixed view of the classical approach to apologetics. On the one hand, he strongly emphasized the fundamental undeniability of the law of noncontradiction. On the other hand, Carnell rejected traditional arguments for God's existence, such as Thomas Aquinas's five ways, and he endorsed David Hume's skeptical objections to those arguments. Instead, Carnell advocated integrating rationalist and evidentialist epistemologies in a criterion he called systematic consistency, internal lack of contradiction in one's belief combined with external agreement with all the facts of one's experience. Using this standard, Christianity may be tested as the "hypothesis" that the God revealed in Scripture exists. In some ways, Carnell speaks of testing this "hypothesis" as one would test any scientific claim, but he qualifies this perspective by noting that this particular hypothesis is an "ultimate postulate" that must be assumed in order to understand the world. Here Carnell displays some indebtedness to both Van Til and Clark while proposing a somewhat different approach.

Carnell's apologetic thought was much richer than this brief survey of part of his *Introduction* might suggest. His approach influenced many other evangelical apologists, notably Gordon Lewis, whose textbook on apologetics we will discuss later (chapter 24).

By Carnell

Carnell, Edward John. *An Introduction to Christian Apologetics: A Philosophic Defense of the Trinitarian-Theistic Faith*. Grand Rapids: Eerdmans, 1948; 4th ed., 1953.

——————. *Christian Commitment: An Apologetic*. New York: Macmillan, 1957.

——————. *The Kingdom of Love and the Pride of Life*. Grand Rapids: Eerdmans, 1960.

——————. *A Philosophy of the Christian Religion*. Grand Rapids: Eerdmans, 1952.

About Carnell

Harper, Kenneth C. "Edward John Carnell: An Evaluation of his Apologetics." *Journal of the Evangelical Theological Society* 20.2 (June 1977): 133–46. One of the few notable periodical articles on Carnell's apologetics. As of this writing, Harper's article is available free online.

Marsden, George M. *Reforming Fundamentalism: Fuller Seminary and the New Evangelicalism.* Grand Rapids: Eerdmans, 1987. This Christian historian's study provides some helpful background context to Carnell's life and work.

18

CORNELIUS VAN TIL

The Defense of the Faith (1955)

> We do not first defend theism philosophically by an appeal to reason and experience in order, after that, to turn to Scripture for our knowledge and defense of Christianity. We get our theism as well as our Christianity from the Bible. —Cornelius Van Til, *The Defense of the Faith*, 24.

Arguably the most controversial apologist of the twentieth century was Cornelius Van Til (1895–1987), a Dutch-American Calvinist whose system of thought is often called presuppositionalism. In 1929 J. Gresham Machen founded Westminster Theological Seminary as a conservative alternative to the recently liberal Princeton Theological Seminary, and the next year brought Van Til, who had earned his degrees at Princeton, to Westminster as its first professor of apologetics. Van Til served in that capacity until his retirement in 1972.

For Van Til, traditional apologetics suffered from being founded on a faulty theological basis. This explains the structure of his major textbook on apologetics, *The Defense of the Faith*. It begins with a chapter on Christian theology and three chapters elucidating "the Christian philosophy" of reality, knowledge, and behavior, before turning to the subject of apologetics proper. Chapters 5 and 7 both critique the Roman Catholic, evangelical (or Arminian), and less consistently Calvinist approaches to apologetics, all of which he finds are theologically compromised to some extent. The last fault, inconsistent Calvinism, belonged to the apologetical tradition at Old Princeton. In Van Til's view, its great mistake was in using rationalistic arguments that concluded that the truths of Christianity are *probably* true. Van Til thought probabilistic arguments detracted from the absolute authority of Scripture as the word of God.

According to Van Til, a Reformed or Calvinistic theology required an equally distinctive Reformed apologetic. This apologetic would not attempt to prove or substantiate Christianity by a simple appeal to factual evidence, as though non-Christians were honest enough to examine the evidence fairly. Instead it would, as Van Til puts it in chapter 6, reason or argue "by presupposition." The first step in this approach is to show that non-Christian systems of thought are incapable of accounting for rationality and morality. Here the apologist is to show that ultimately all non-Christian systems of thought fall into irrationalism. The second step is to commend the Christian view as giving the only possible presuppositional foundation for thought and life. For Van Til this is the *only* legitimate apologetic approach: "The best, the only, the absolutely certain proof of the truth of Christianity is that unless its truth be presupposed there is no proof of anything. Christianity is proved as being the very foundation of the idea of proof itself" (396).

Van Til's students have included some of the most influential apologists of a more broadly evangelical perspective, most notably Edward John Carnell, whom we introduced in the previous chapter, and Francis Schaeffer, whom we will introduce later (chapter 21). Van Til did not, however, regard either of these students of his as sound proponents of a Reformed apologetic, and he wrote extensive critiques of their apologetic thought. (Carnell receives some criticism in *The Defense of the Faith*.) Although much of Van Til's criticism of other apologists was divisive, it also led to much fruitful discussion and reflection on apologetic method.

By Van Til

Van Til, Cornelius. *A Christian Theory of Knowledge*. Phillipsburg, NJ: Presbyterian & Reformed, 1969. The standard presuppositionalist survey of the history of Christian philosophy and apologetics, giving special attention to the church fathers, Roman Catholic thought, the differences between Abraham Kuyper and B. B. Warfield, and J. Oliver Buswell's apologetic.

_____. *Apologetics*. 2nd ed. William Edgar, ed. Phillipsburg, NJ: Presbyterian & Reformed, 2003. Reprint of the 1976 edition with explanatory footnotes.

_____. *The Defense of the Faith*. Philadelphia: Presbyterian & Reformed, 1955; 3rd ed., 1967; 4th ed., ed. K. Scott Oliphint, 2008. The fourth edition restores material that had been removed in the 1967 edition and adds explanatory footnotes. Page numbers cited in this chapter are from the first edition.

About Van Til

Bahnsen, Greg L. *Van Til's Apologetic: Readings and Analysis* (Phillipsburg, NJ: Presbyterian & Reformed, 1998. A thorough, detailed work combining readings from Van Til's books arranged thematically with Bahnsen's own exposition and defense of Van Til's arguments.

Frame, John M. *Cornelius Van Til: An Analysis of His Thought.* Phillipsburg, NJ: Presbyterian & Reformed, 1995. Frame, a presuppositionalist, offers a clear, thoughtful explanation of Van Til's positions, while also presenting a more positive assessment of the thought of classical and evidentialist apologists than the assessment of his teacher Van Til.

19

JOHN C. WHITCOMB JR. & HENRY M. MORRIS

The Genesis Flood (1961)

The instructed Christian knows that the evidences for full divine inspiration of Scripture are far weightier than the evidence is for any fact of science. —John C. Whitcomb Jr. and Henry M. Morris, *The Genesis Flood*, 118.

In 1953, Henry Morris (1918–2006), a professor of hydraulics engineering, presented a paper on "Biblical Evidence for a Recent Creation and Universal Deluge" to the American Scientific Affiliation meeting at Grace Theological Seminary. John Whitcomb (1924–), who had been teaching for two years there, heard Morris and changed his view of Genesis from the gap theory to young-earth creationism. Whitcomb did his Th.D. dissertation at Grace on "The Genesis Flood" (1957). He and Morris then teamed up to write a book with the same title, combining their theological and scientific interests to produce a defense of a global, catastrophic Flood in keeping with a literal reading of Genesis.

Up to this point, the most significant defenses of this position had been written by Seventh-day Adventists, notably George McCready Price. *The Genesis Flood*, by a

Grace Brethren theologian and a Southern Baptist scientist, enjoyed widespread acceptance among evangelicals, eventually selling over 300,000 copies. Although both Morris and Whitcomb were important Christian apologists, our focus here is primarily on Whitcomb, who laid the philosophical and theological foundation for the modern young-earth creationist apologetic.

Although Cornelius Van Til is not mentioned in *The Genesis Flood*, in later publications Whitcomb made clear that he based his view of the relationship between science and Scripture on a form of Van Til's apologetic system. Like Van Til, Whitcomb emphasized the impossibility of scientific theories without religious presuppositions. He argued that both creationism and evolutionism should be seen as essentially religious in character. "Our conclusions must unavoidably be colored by our Biblical presuppositions, and this we plainly acknowledge. But uniformitarian scholarship is no less bound by its own presuppositions and these are quite as dogmatic as those of our own" (xxi).

For Whitcomb, the Bible speaks both more authoritatively and more clearly about such questions as the age of the universe than science should or can. "The instructed Christian knows that the evidences for full divine inspiration of Scripture are far weightier than the evidence is for any fact of science" (118). They do not say here what those weightier "evidences" are, but clearly, they cannot come from "any fact of science."

The basic thesis of *The Genesis Flood* is that geological uniformitarianism was an unbelieving presupposition that had prejudiced most geologists and even many Christian scholars to the clear teaching of a global Flood in Genesis. In the first four chapters, Whitcomb defends the global Flood as the teaching of Genesis and argues against compromise views such as a global yet tranquil flood or a local flood. In chapters 5 through 7, which comprise about two-thirds of the book, Morris presents an interpretation of the geological evidence that he argues is consistent with Genesis, the heart of which is the principle of "appearance of age."

The Genesis Flood is widely credited as having launched the modern creation science movement. Morris went on to establish the Institute for Creation Research, which for many years was the leading organization promoting young-earth creationism. It is certainly one of the most influential books in apologetics of the twentieth century.

By Whitcomb

Whitcomb, John C. *The Early Earth: An Introduction to Biblical Creationism.* 3rd ed. Winona Lake, IN: BMH Books, 2011. Perhaps Whitcomb's best-known book other than *The Genesis Flood.*

_____. "Remembering *The Genesis Flood.*" Answers in Genesis, 2010. Whitcomb's recollections of the events leading to him writing the book with Morris.

_____, and Henry M. Morris. *The Genesis Flood: The Biblical Record and Its Scientific Implications.* Phillipsburg, NJ: Presbyterian & Reformed, 1961. A 50th Anniversary Edition (2011) includes a new eight-page preface.

About Whitcomb

Numbers, Ronald L. *The Creationists: From Scientific Creationism to Intelligent Design*. Expanded ed. Cambridge, MA: Harvard University Press, 2006. A remarkable history of the movement acknowledged as objective by both creationists (including Whitcomb and Morris) and non-creationists. Includes an entire chapter on *The Genesis Flood*.

www.whitcombministries.org. John Whitcomb's ministry website.

20

GORDON H. CLARK

The Philosophy of Science and Belief in God (1964)

> Anti-Christian arguments based on science always depend on premises that will soon be discarded. —Gordon H. Clark, *The Philosophy of Science and Belief in God*, 102.

Gordon H. Clark (1902–1985) is one of the two most influential advocates of a presuppositional approach to apologetics, the other being Cornelius Van Til, whom we introduced earlier (chapter 18). From 1945 to 1973, Clark was chairman of the philosophy department at Butler University in Indianapolis.

Clark's *deductive* presuppositionalism is subtly but significantly different from Van Til's. According to Van Til, truth is found everywhere in God's world, but this truth can be known only because God has given us the capacity to know it. By contrast, Clark maintained that all that could truly be known was to be found in Scripture itself. In his view, knowledge of truth requires deductive proof, and nothing can be deduced from the uncertain facts of the natural world or of the human mind. Furthermore, inductive reasoning is unreliable, because inductive arguments are formally fallacious. The only source of indisputable premises with which logic can work is the Bible. So, Clark argued, the infallible statements of Scripture provide the only source of certain knowledge, and only what the Bible actually says, or what can be logically deduced from those biblical statements, constitutes real knowledge.

Clark works out what this all means for science in *The Philosophy of Science and Belief in God*, in which he argues that science cannot arrive at truth. Although we can ascertain facts about the physical world, science cannot *explain* any of these facts (36). Worse still, "laws of nature" are not descriptions of the way things actually are in the real world. Rather, they are mathematical idealizations. Clark does not mince words: "Therefore, all the laws of physics are false" (60).

On the basis of this line of reasoning, Clark favors a form of the philosophy of science known as operationalism, a version of nonrealism, according to which science does not progress toward more accurate knowledge of the "real" world. According to operationalism, science consists in descriptions of the *operations* performed by the scientist, not actual entities or realities. "Electrons and light waves are not physically existing things; they are elements of a set of instructions on how to operate in a laboratory" (90).

In Clark's apologetic, operationalism completely undermines any attempt to use science to disprove creation or any other aspect of Christian doctrine. If science is not *true*, it cannot prove Christianity false. Since science develops protocols for performing operations in a laboratory, its "laws" are merely conventions that can be discarded for new ones. "Therefore anti-Christian arguments based on science always depend on premises that will soon be discarded" (102). For Clark, then, science really is irrelevant to Christian apologetics. "From this the further conclusion follows that science can never disprove the truth of Christianity. It can never prove or disprove any metaphysical or theological assertion" (109).

Most Christians will probably not find Clark's philosophy of science persuasive. Yet it demonstrates the need for Christians to engage such questions. Clark's book was one of the first to do so.

By Clark

Clark, Gordon H. "Apologetics." In *Contemporary Evangelical Thought*, ed. Carl F. H. Henry. Great Neck, NY: Channel Press, 1957.

_____. *A Christian View of Men and Things: An Introduction to Philosophy*. Grand Rapids: Eerdmans, 1952; reprint, Grand Rapids: Baker, 1981. One of Clark's most respected works, presenting his approach to history, science, religion, epistemology, and other areas of thought.

_____. *The Philosophy of Science and Belief in God*. 3rd ed. Jefferson, Md.: Trinity Foundation, 1996.

_____. *Religion, Reason and Revelation*. Nutley, NJ: Craig Press, 1961; 2nd ed. Jefferson, MD: Trinity Foundation, 1986. Notable for Clark's treatment of the relationship of faith and reason, his critique of the cosmological argument, and his argument for a deterministic solution to the problem of evil.

About Clark

http://gordonhclark.reformed.info/. The website of The Gordon H. Clark Foundation.

Nash, Ronald H., ed. *The Philosophy of Gordon H. Clark: A Festschrift*. Philadelphia: Presbyterian & Reformed, 1968; 2nd ed., Jefferson, MD: Trinity Foundation, 1992. Collection of essays in honor of Clark, including by apologists who were critical of his views, such as John Warwick Montgomery.

Robbins, John W. "An Introduction to Gordon H. Clark." *Trinity Review*, July/Aug. 1993. Online at http://www.trinity-foundation.org/journal.php?id=192. Overview of Clark's life and thought by a passionate advocate of Clark's system of thought.

21

FRANCIS A. SCHAEFFER IV
The God Who Is There (1968)

> Christianity begins with "In the beginning God created the heavens (the total of the cosmos) and the earth." That is the answer to the twentieth century and its lostness. At this point we are then ready to explain the second lostness (the original cause of all lostness) and the answer in the death of Christ. —Francis A. Schaeffer, *The God Who Is There*, 181.

Francis Schaeffer (1912–1984) was one of the most beloved Christian apologists of the twentieth century. *Newsweek* once called him "the guru of fundamentalism." Schaeffer studied for a time under Cornelius Van Til, who was still developing his presuppositional apologetic. In 1948 Francis and his wife Edith moved to Switzerland to serve as missionaries. During the next few years young people began coming to Schaeffer's home to discuss their doubts and to learn about Christianity. As they returned home, they spread the word, and soon the Schaeffers found themselves engaged full-time in personal evangelism and apologetics from their home, which they called *l'Abri* ("the Shelter"), to people from all over the world.

Beginning in the 1960s Francis was invited to speak at conferences and at leading colleges and universities in Europe and America. Out of his lectures were developed his most influential books, beginning with *Escape from Reason* and *The God Who Is There*, both of which were published in 1968. Schaeffer regarded these two books and his 1972 book *He Is There and He Is Not Silent* as a trilogy (later published together in volume 1 of his *Complete Works*, cited here) that formed the foundation of his published work. We will focus on *The God Who Is There*.

Schaeffer's method integrated elements of classical, evidential, and presuppositional apologetics. As in classical apologetics, he advocated a two-stage defense that moves from God as Creator to Christ as Savior. "We must never forget that the first part of the gospel is not 'Accept Christ as Savior,' but 'God is there'" (144). Lack of belief in "the God who is there" has led to the loss of meaning for modern people. As in evidentialism, Schaeffer asserted that Scripture invites reasoned scrutiny by making claims about "the cosmos and history, which are open to verification" (120). Yet he cautioned that reason and evidence need to be employed with an awareness of the assumptions people bring to any discussion. What he called "presuppositional apologetics" (7) involves helping non-Christians to see that they cannot live in a manner consistent with their presuppositions, according to which life has no real meaning. The Christian needs to get to know the non-Christian well enough to help him find his "point of tension" (129–35) between what he believes and how he lives. We can do so by lovingly helping him discover the logical implications of what he says he believes—an apologetic strategy that Schaeffer calls "taking the roof off" (140).

Schaeffer did not advocate any one school of apologetic theory because "each person must be dealt with as an individual, not as a case or statistic or machine" (130). "I do not believe that there is any one system of apologetics that meets the need of all people, any more than I think there is any one form of evangelism that meets the need of all people. It is to be shaped on the basis of love for the person as a person" (177).

By Schaeffer

Schaeffer, Francis A. *The Complete Works of Francis A. Schaeffer.* 5 vols. Westchester, IL: Crossway Books, 1982. There are, of course, other editions of his books.

About Schaeffer

Barrs, Jerram. "Francis Schaeffer: The Man and His Message." *Reformation 21: The Online Magazine of the Alliance of Confessing Evangelicals,* Nov. 2006. This article is currently online at https://www.covenantseminary.edu/francis-schaeffer-the-man-and-his-message/.

Morris, Thomas V. *Francis Schaeffer's Apologetics: A Critique.* 2nd ed. Grand Rapids: Baker, 1987. Original edition, 1976.

Ruegsegger, Ronald W., ed. *Reflections on Francis Schaeffer.* Grand Rapids: Zondervan, 1986.

https://library.sebts.edu/schaeffer/home. The Francis A. Schaeffer Society at Southeastern Baptist Theological

Seminary, which also maintains the collection of Schaeffer's personal papers.

www.theschaefferfoundation.com. The website of the Francis A. Schaeffer Foundation, which was co-founded by Schaeffer's widow Edith.

22

JOHN WARWICK MONTGOMERY
History and Christianity (1971)

To be skeptical of the resultant text of the New Testament
books is to allow all of classical antiquity to slip into obscurity,
for no documents of the ancient period are as well attested bib-
liographically as the New Testament. —John Warwick Montgomery, *History and Christianity*, 29.

John Warwick Montgomery (1931–) is a sophisticated
Christian scholar who has made significant contributions
to law, theology, and apologetics for almost sixty years. He
earned at least nine degrees in a variety of fields (philosophy, library science, theology, and canon law) and creden-
tials for practicing law in California, England, and France.
Montgomery had opportunities to share the gospel with
such world-famous figures as Anwar Sadat, Tony Blair,
and Princess Diana, and he famously engaged in debates
over the years with several atheists as well as a liberal bishop and a Muslim apologist.

Montgomery's 1963 debate with philosopher Avrum
Stroll at the University of British Columbia led eventually to the publication of his popular little book *History and
Christianity*. In it he set forth a model of evidentialist apologetics. The first step is to defend the biblical writings, not

as infallible Scripture, but as historically credible and reliable documents. Securing belief in God is not considered a prerequisite to taking this first step; only clearing away any methodological or philosophical assumptions that prejudge the question of the truth of the biblical narratives is necessary. Hence, Montgomery detailed "four common errors" in Stroll's anti-Christian polemic before beginning his apologetic proper: relying on rationalist "authorities," ignoring the evidence from Paul, assuming that miracles cannot happen, and substituting speculation for facts (17–22).

Having cleared away these errors, Montgomery began his positive case, in which he proposed to treat the New Testament writings "as we would any other historical materials" (26). To this end, he employed tests of reliability drawn from a textbook on English literary history by a military historian. Montgomery and other evidentialists regularly use these "bibliographical," "internal," and "external" tests to defend the historical reliability of the New Testament. He argued that the New Testament documents have been more reliably preserved than any other ancient literature, that the Gospels' internal claims to historicity are consistent and to be given the benefit of the doubt, and that external information from the early church about the origins of the Gospels confirms their reliability (29–32). Montgomery concluded that "the New Testament documents must be regarded as reliable sources of information" (43).

The next step in Montgomery's argument, drawing heavily here on C. S. Lewis, was to show that the various New Testament writers all attest that "Jesus regarded himself as no less than God in the flesh" (49). Proceeding chronologically, Montgomery surveyed Paul, Mark, Matthew, Luke, and John, concluding that these present a "consistent portrait of Jesus" as having claimed to be divine (57). From there, he argued that Jesus was neither a charlatan nor a lunatic (61–66). For the skeptic, this leaves only the supposition that Jesus never made such claims and that his disciples deified him. In response, Montgomery showed that first-century Jewish thought provided no plausible context in which the disciples would ever have considered deifying their dead teacher (66–72). What convinced them, he concluded, was Jesus' resurrection (72–78).

John Warwick Montgomery, still living as of the time of this writing, is one of the most significant Christian apologists of the past fifty years. Almost every evangelical apologist today who engages in the defense of the historical reliability of the New Testament has been influenced directly or indirectly by Montgomery's teaching.

By Montgomery

Montgomery, John Warwick. *Always Be Ready: A Primer on Defending the Christian Faith*. Irvine, CA: 1517 Publishing, 2017.

_____. *Defending the Gospel in Legal Style: Essays on Legal Apologetics & the Justification of Classical Christian Faith*. Eugene, OR: Wipf & Stock, 2017.

_____. *Faith Founded on Fact: Essays in Evidential Apologetics*. Nashville: Thomas Nelson, 1978.

_____. *Fighting the Good Fight: A Life in Defense of the Faith.* Christliche Philosophie heute / Christian Philosophy Today 17. Quomodo Philosophia Christianorum Hodie Estimatur. Eugene, OR: Wipf & Stock, 2016. Montgomery's autobiography makes for fascinating reading.

_____. *History and Christianity.* Downers Grove, IL: InterVarsity, 1971; reprint, Minneapolis: Bethany, 1986.

_____. *History, Law, and Christianity.* With a commendatory letter from C. S. Lewis. Irvine, CA: NRP Books, 2014. Includes *History and Christianity* and other material.

_____. *Tractatus Logico-Theologicus.* Christliche Philosophie heute 1. 5th ed., rev. Bonn: Verlag für Kultur und Wissenschaft, 2012. Montgomery's most rigorous apologetic text, appealing to "historical, jurisprudential, and scientific standards of evidence."

About Montgomery

https://www.jwm.christendom.co.uk/. Montgomery's official website.

https://www.johnwarwickmontgomery.com/. Montgomery's Apologetics Academy.

Clifford, Ross. *John Warwick Montgomery's Legal Apologetic: An Apologetic for All Seasons.* Christliche Philosophie heute 5. Eugene, OR: Wipf and Stock, 2016.

_____. "Justification of the Legal Apologetic of John Warwick Montgomery: An Apologetic for All Seasons." *Global Journal of Classic Theology: An Online Journal of Evangelical Theology* 3/1 (April 2002). Online at www.globaljournalct.com.

Dembski, William, and Thomas Schirrmacher, eds. *Tough-Minded Christianity: Honoring the Legacy of John Warwick Montgomery*. Nashville: B&H, 2008. Essays explicating and defending Montgomery's apologetic method and covering worldviews, nature, doctrine, apologetics, and law, ethics, and society, with contributions by noted Christian scholars. Includes a bibliography of Montgomery's works through 2008.

23

NORMAN L. GEISLER
Christian Apologetics (1976)

We offer the claim that theism is the only adequate world view. All others are self-defeating or actually unaffirmable. Only theism is actually undeniable. It offers an argument with undeniable premises that leads inescapably to the existence of an infinitely perfect and powerful Being beyond this world who is the current sustaining cause of all finite, changing, and contingent beings. —Norman L. Geisler, *Christian Apologetics*, 258.

Norman Geisler (1932–2019) authored, co-authored, and edited nearly a hundred books on apologetics, philosophy of religion, ethics, theology, and biblical studies, making him a key figure in evangelicalism. A philosopher by training, Geisler taught apologetics and theology at several major evangelical seminaries for over fifty years. He co-founded Southern Evangelical Seminary in Matthews, North Carolina, in 1992, and Veritas International University in Santa Ana, California, in 2008. Geisler was also well known for his criticisms of various evangelical scholars over the years whose views he found to compromise evangelical views of Scripture or the nature of God.

Although Geisler was theologically an evangelical Protestant, in philosophy and apologetics he was a convinced Thomist (advocate of the approach of Thomas Aquinas). His approach to apologetics proceeded in two steps. First, the apologist builds a case for theism by demonstrating how it conforms to rational criteria used to evaluate the truth claims of competing worldviews. Having shown that theism is true according to these criteria, the apologist may then present the evidence for the historical truth claims of Christianity. Geisler set out this method in full in his 1976 textbook *Christian Apologetics*, which is divided into three parts: apologetic method, theistic apologetics (the first step), and Christian apologetics (the second step).

In Part One, Geisler evaluated seven epistemological approaches to the question of God and concluded that they have inadequate tests for truth. In their place he proposed that for worldviews *unaffirmability* should be the test for falsehood and *undeniability* the test for truth. Unaffirmability occurs when a statement is directly or indirectly self-defeating, whereas undeniability applies to statements that are definitional, tautologous, or existentially self-confirming.

In Part Two, Geisler argued that only theism is affirmable and undeniable. He examined competing worldviews (deism, pantheism, panentheism, atheism) and argues that they all fail the test for truth. He then presented a cosmological argument with undeniable premises (something exists; nothing comes from nothing) "that leads inescapably to the existence of an infinitely perfect and powerful Being beyond this world who is the current sustaining cause of all finite, changing, and contingent beings" (258).

In Part Three, Geisler argued that Christianity is the true theistic religion. Since he was shifting from judging among worldviews to judging among theistic religions, he moved away from the criteria of unaffirmability and undeniability to the probabilistic criterion of systematic consistency (comprehensiveness, adequacy, consistency, coherence). Geisler argued that given the truth of theism, miracles are possible, and we can know that they have occurred in history. From these premises Geisler proceeded to make the case for Christianity. He argued that the New Testament writings are authentic and reliable, and then he applied historical methods to those documents to show that Jesus Christ claimed to be God and that he vindicated this claim by fulfilling Old Testament prophecies and rising from the dead. The most systematically consistent interpretation of these facts is that Christ was, in truth, the Son of God. Finally, Geisler argued that on the basis of Christ's divine authority, we should accept Christ's teaching that Scripture is the word of God.

By Geisler

Geisler, Norman L. *Baker Encyclopedia of Christian Apologetics.* Grand Rapids: Baker, 1999. Geisler's magnum opus, with entries (often quite substantive) on a host of issues, persons, and movements of relevance to apologetics.

_____. *Christian Apologetics.* Grand Rapids: Baker, 1976. Geisler's foundational apologetics textbook.

_____, and Winfried Corduan. *Philosophy of Religion.* 2nd ed. Grand Rapids: Baker, 1988. One of Geisler's best books that he co-authored with another evangelical scholar.

_____, with Frank Turek. *I Don't Have Enough Faith to Be an Atheist*. Foreword by David Limbaugh. Wheaton, IL: Good News Publishers—Crossway Books, 2004. Geisler's most popular book, co-authored with Frank Turek, now one of the most popular Christian apologists in America.

About Geisler

Beckwith, Francis J., William Lane Craig, and J. P. Moreland, eds. *To Everyone an Answer: A Case for the Christian Worldview: Essays in Honor of Norman L. Geisler*. Downers Grove, IL: InterVarsity Press, 2004. Contributions by many leading 21st-century evangelical apologists such as Paul Copan, William Lane Craig, Douglas Groothuis, Gary Habermas, Craig Hazen, Greg Koukl, J. P. Moreland, Ravi Zacharias, and others.

Miethe, Terry L., ed. *I Am Put Here for the Defense of the Gospel: Dr. Norman L. Geisler: A* Festschrift *in His Honor*. Eugene, OR: Wipf & Stock, 2016. Essays on apologetics, biblical studies, philosophy, ethics, and other religions, many of them by Geisler's students.

normangeisler.com. Geisler's website, which includes links to schools and other organizations with which he was associated.

24

GORDON R. LEWIS

Testing Christianity's Truth Claims (1976)

From Cornelius Van Til at Westminster Theological Seminary he [Edward John Carnell] took his starting point, the existence of the triune God of the Bible. However, this tenet is not an unquestioned presupposition for Carnell, but a hypothesis to be tested. His test of truth is threefold. At Wheaton College in the classes of Gordon H. Clark, Carnell found the test of non-contradiction. The test of fitness to empirical fact was championed by Edgar S. Brightman at Boston University where Carnell earned his Ph.D. The requirement of relevance to personal experience became prominent during Carnell's Th.D. research at Harvard University in Sören Kierkegaard and Reinhold Niebuhr. —Gordon R. Lewis, *Testing Christianity's Truth Claims*, 176.

The rise of differing apologetic methods and theories in the first half of the twentieth century was bound to result in the publication of textbooks surveying these competing views. The earliest seems to have been Bernard Ramm's *Types of Apologetic Systems* (1953), drastically rewritten later as *Varieties of Christian Apologetics* (1962). The most successful such textbook in the twentieth century, however, was Gordon Lewis's *Testing Christianity's Truth Claims:*

Approaches to Christian Apologetics. Lewis (1926–2016) taught philosophy, theology, and apologetics at Denver Seminary from 1958 to 1993. In 1984, Lewis founded Evangelical Ministries to New Religions (EMNR), a fellowship of such individuals and organizations.

Lewis's book not only surveyed the apologetic methods of noteworthy modern apologists but also advocated integrating those methods. His integrative approach was consciously modeled on that developed by Edward John Carnell, whom we profiled earlier (chapter 17). After an introductory chapter, Lewis offered one chapter each on five apologists followed by four chapters on Carnell. The purpose of the book was to show that what Lewis called Carnell's "verificational approach" brings together the valid elements of the other approaches. They are, Lewis said, "like separate pieces of a stained glass window" that Carnell "sought to put…back together" (176).

Lewis's first apologist is J. Oliver Buswell Jr., whom he described as advocating "pure empiricism." His approach, according to Lewis, uses "the test of objective evidence" (45). Next, Lewis examined "rational empiricism" as a system that employs "the test of objective evidence and logical thought-forms" (76). Lewis divided his attention in this chapter equally between Hackett and Floyd E. Hamilton.

In the following two chapters Lewis considered the "rationalism" of Gordon H. Clark, who used "the test of logical consistency" (100), and the "biblical authoritarianism" of Cornelius Van Til, who used "the test of scriptural authority" (125). Clark made logic primary and argues that the Bible provides the only logically consistent system of knowledge, while Van Til made the Bible primary and argues that our use of logic must be subordinated to the Bible. Lewis emphasized the differences between their two methods, which are indeed quite significant. Of course, Clark's system is just as much one of "biblical authoritarianism" as Van Til's.

Lewis turned next to the "mysticism" of Earl E. Barrett as an example of a system utilizing "the test of personal experience" (151). Warren C. Young is also cited at length as an advocate of this approach. These two apologists are not well known today, but they were evangelical professors at Midwest schools in the mid-twentieth century who emphasized personal encounter with God in their apologetics.

In the remainder of the book, Lewis expounded on Carnell's approach and argued that it combined the strengths of the other approaches. In the appendix, Lewis profiled Francis Schaeffer, Bernard Ramm, C. S. Lewis, and several other apologists, showing that they took approaches similar to Carnell's. Gordon Lewis's irenic analysis has encouraged numerous Christians to learn from the contributions of apologists of varying methods.

By Gordon Lewis

Lewis, Gordon R. *Testing Christianity's Truth Claims: Approaches to Christian Apologetics.* Chicago: Moody, 1976.

_____, and Bruce A. Demarest. *Integrative Theology.* 3 vols. Grand Rapids: Zondervan, 1996. Unusual (and very well done) theology textbook, treating each traditional subject area in theology under the categories of historical, biblical, systematic, apologetic, and practical theology.

About Gordon Lewis

Groothuis, Douglas. "Gordon Lewis: Irenic Apologist." *Christianity Today*, June 17, 2016. Groothuis, an evangelical philosopher and apologist, and a younger colleague of Lewis, was the ideal person to write an article following the passing of Lewis.

25

ALVIN PLANTINGA
Faith and Rationality (1983)

> Perhaps the main function of apologetics is to show that from
> a philosophical point of view, Christians and other theists have
> nothing whatever for which to apologize. —Alvin Plantinga,
> "Reason and Belief in God," in *Faith and Rationality*, 33.

Alvin Plantinga (1932–) taught at Calvin College from
1963 to 1982, then at the University of Notre Dame until
2010, when he returned to Calvin College (now Calvin
University). He has served as president of both the Society of Christian Philosophers (which he helped found)
and the American Philosophical Association. In addition
to his Ph.D. from Yale, Plantinga holds six honorary degrees, was a Guggenheim Fellow, and in 2017 received
the Templeton Prize. Like Cornelius Van Til, another
Dutch-American Calvinist, Plantinga sought to develop an approach to apologetics grounded in Reformed
thought. Plantinga's way of doing this, however, was quite
different from Van Til's.

In 1983, the year after Plantinga left Calvin for Notre
Dame, the latter's university press published a book of es-
says edited by Plantinga and a Calvin associate, Nicholas
Wolterstorff, with essays by other Reformed philosophers.

The book, *Faith and Rationality: Reason and Belief in God*, had a profound impact, not only in Christian apologetics, but also in the halls of academia. Plantinga's lengthy contribution "Reason and Belief in God," in particular, changed the direction of philosophy of religion in universities and colleges around the world. Books and articles began appearing every year discussing the merits of Plantinga's "Reformed Epistemology," as it came to be known. Plantinga's *magnum opus* is a three-volume series of books: *Warrant: The Current Debate* and *Warrant and Proper Function* (both 1993) and *Warranted Christian Belief* (2000). Here we summarize Plantinga's 1983 essay that launched the Reformed Epistemology movement.

According to Plantinga, a belief is "basic" if a person holds it without basing it on some other belief, that is, if it is not inferred from other beliefs. A belief is "properly basic" if the person holding it is in some significant way warranted in doing so. The fact that a belief is basic for someone does not mean it is *groundless*. For example, a person's belief that he sees a tree is basic because it is not inferred from other beliefs; but it is not groundless, because it is grounded in his immediate experience of seeing the tree. Likewise, a person who holds as a basic belief that God exists might do so because he had a religious experience; that experience, then, would be the ground of the belief. Plantinga insisted that belief in God could be properly basic for him without being groundless.

In perhaps the most memorable part of his essay, Plantinga anticipated and answered what he called "the

Great Pumpkin objection": "What about the belief that the Great Pumpkin returns every Halloween? Could I properly take *that* as basic?" (74). Plantinga's answer was no, because that belief would have nothing to ground it, and there is no reason why anyone should consider such a belief basic (74–78). A belief held as basic can even be challenged by evidences or reasons that Plantinga called "defeaters," which themselves need to be defeated for a person to continue being warranted in his belief. Plantinga's Reformed Epistemology, then, is not opposed to apologetics.

By Plantinga

Plantinga, Alvin. "A Christian Life Partly Lived." In *Philosophers Who Believe: The Spiritual Journeys of 11 Leading Thinkers*, ed. Kelly James Clark, 45–82. Downers Grove, IL: InterVarsity, 1993. Autobiographical reflections from earlier in Plantinga's long career.

_____. *Knowledge and Christian Belief*. Grand Rapids: Eerdmans, 2015. Short distillation of the argument advanced in more detail in *Warranted Christian Belief*.

_____. *Warrant and Proper Function*. New York: Oxford University Press, 1993.

_____. *Warrant: The Current Debate*. New York: Oxford University Press, 1993.

_____. *Warranted Christian Belief*. New York: Oxford University Press, 2000. Third of the three-volume series on warrant in epistemology (the philosophical study of knowledge), Plantinga's magnum opus.

_____, and Nicholas Wolterstorff, eds. *Faith and Rationality: Reason and Belief in God.* Notre Dame, IN: University of Notre Dame Press, 1983. Includes the essay, "Reason and Belief in God" (16–93).

About Plantinga

Clark, Kelly James. *Return to Reason: A Critique of Enlightenment Evidentialism and a Defense of Reason and Belief in God.* Grand Rapids: Eerdmans, 1990. Excellent introduction to Plantinga's approach to apologetics.

Mascord, Keith A. *Alvin Plantinga and Christian Apologetics.* Eugene, OR: Wipf & Stock, 2006. Anglican scholar in Australia analyzes and assesses Plantinga's contributions to and perspectives on apologetics. Endorsed by Plantinga himself.

26

WILLIAM LANE CRAIG
Apologetics: An Introduction (1984)

> We *know* Christianity is true primarily by the self-authenticating witness of the Holy Spirit. We *show* Christianity is true by demonstrating that it is systematically consistent. —William Lane Craig, *Reasonable Faith: Christian Truth and Apologetics*, 48.

William Lane Craig (1949–) is an evangelical scholar at the forefront of apologetics today. He earned doctorates in philosophy of religion (Birmingham) and theology (Munich). Since 1994 he has been a Research Professor at Biola University. In addition to his publications, Craig is widely known for his many debates with atheists and skeptics. His ministry Reasonable Faith has a popular website and a network of chapters throughout the United States and on every continent. Most academics make their mark in only one area of research, but Craig is a leading evangelical theorist in at least three: the cosmological argument, the attributes of God, and the resurrection of Christ. His apologetics textbook, originally titled *Apologetics: An Introduction* (1984), was later revised as *Reasonable Faith: Christian Truth and Apologetics* (1994, 2008). Citations here are from the 1994 edition.

In regard to the question, "How do I know Christianity is true?" Craig distinguishes between *knowing* that Christianity is true by the witness of the Spirit and *showing* others that Christianity is true by presenting evidence of its systematic consistency. Craig's first step is to "show" that life is absurd without God (chapter 2). This does not mean that we believe in God in an irrational attempt to convince ourselves that life has meaning. Rather, we believe in God because there is proof that he exists. In chapter 3, Craig surveys the traditional arguments for God's existence and finds "quite a number of the proffered theistic arguments to be sound and persuasive and together to constitute a powerful cumulative case for the existence of God" (91–92). His favorite theistic argument is the *kalam* cosmological argument, originally formulated by medieval Arabic Muslim philosophers.

In chapters 4 and 5 Craig argues that miracles are possible and that we can know that they have occurred in history. "Once the non-Christian understands who God is, then the problem of miracles should cease to be a problem for him" (155). Chapter 6, on the historical reliability of the New Testament, is written by Craig Blomberg, a premier evangelical New Testament scholar. In chapter 7, Craig argues that even using only the sayings of Jesus admitted by the extremely liberal Jesus Seminar, one can show that Jesus considered himself to be the divine Son of God. The importance of Jesus' claims to deity is that they "provide the religio-historical context in which the resurrection becomes significant, as it confirms those claims" (253). This leads Craig to the capstone of his apologetic, the historical argument for the resurrection of Jesus (chapter 8). He makes his case based on "the empty tomb, the resurrection appearances, and the origin of the Christian faith" (272).

In the conclusion, Craig says that "the ultimate apologetic" is to show people our love for God and one another (299–301). Good arguments are more likely to receive a hearing from good people.

By Craig

Craig, William Lane. *Assessing the New Testament Evidence for the Historicity of the Resurrection of Jesus*. Studies in the Bible and Early Christianity, vol. 16. Lewiston, N.Y.: Edwin Mellen Press, 1989.

_____. "Classical Apologetics." In *Five Views on Apologetics*, ed. Steven B. Cowan, 26–55. Counterpoint series. Grand Rapids: Zondervan, 2000.

_____. *On Guard: Defending Your Faith with Reason and Precision*. Foreword by Lee Strobel. Colorado Springs: David C. Cook, 2010. Addresses common questions such as "Can we be good without God?" or "Did Jesus rise from the dead?"

_____. *Reasonable Faith: Christian Truth and Apologetics*. Wheaton, IL: Crossway, 1994, 2008. Revised versions of *Apologetics: An Introduction*. Chicago: Moody, 1984.

_____, with Joseph Gorra. *A Reasonable Response: Answers to Tough Questions on God, Christianity, and the Bible*. Chicago: Moody Press, 2013. Addresses more advanced issues on a wide range of questions, in places defending some of Craig's controversial theological positions.

_____, and John Dominic Crossan. *Will the Real Jesus Please Stand Up? A Debate between William Lane Craig and John Dominic Crossan.* Moderated by William F. Buckley Jr.; ed. Paul Copan. With responses from Robert J. Miller, Craig L. Blomberg, Marcus Borg, and Ben Witherington III. Grand Rapids: Baker, 1998. One of the very best published debates on the resurrection of Christ.

_____, and Walter Sinnott-Armstrong. *God? A Debate between a Christian and an Atheist.* Point/Counterpoint Series. James P. Sterba, series ed. New York: Oxford University Press, 2004. One of several of Craig's debates with atheists.

www.reasonablefaith.org. The website of Craig's ministry, Reasonable Faith, one of the most popular apologetics ministries today.

About Craig

Kristof, Nicholas. "Professor, Was Jesus Really Born to a Virgin? I question William Lane Craig of Talbot School of Theology and Houston Baptist University about Christianity." *New York Times*, Dec. 21, 2018. Kristof is skeptical, but kudos to him and the *Times* for giving Craig an opportunity to be heard.

Schneider, Nathan. "The New Theist: How William Lane Craig Became Christian Philosophy's Boldest Apostle." *Chronicle of Higher Education*, July 1, 2013. Long, generally positive article in a rather surprising place.

"Who Is William Lane Craig?" BeThinking.org, 2011. Nice overview of Craig's life, work, books, and debate.

27

J. P. MORELAND
Scaling the Secular City (1987)

> Some people cannot see God at work in the world or under-
> stand and appropriate certain features of the Bible because they
> have not been trained to see those patterns. Instead, they view
> the world through secular glasses. Their subconscious structures
> cause them to interpret events and statements in ways which
> stifle growth. Apologetics can focus attention on some of those
> secular structures, call them into question, and release the self
> to view the world in a way more compatible with a Christian
> worldview. —J. P. Moreland, *Scaling the Secular City,* 12.

James Porter ("J. P.") Moreland (1948–) has been a professor of philosophy at Talbot School of Theology, part
of Biola University, since 1990. He earned degrees in
science, theology, and philosophy, making him unusu-
ally well prepared to address a wide range of topics in
Christian apologetics. His multidisciplinary compe-
tency was on full display in *Scaling the Secular City: A
Defense of Christianity,* published just three years before
he joined the Talbot faculty. At the beginning of the book
(10), Moreland acknowledges his indebtedness to two of
the apologists we have considered, Norman Geisler (who
also wrote the Foreword) and William Lane Craig (see
chapters 23 and 26). Moreland regards the evidence he

presents in the book as showing that belief in the Christian God is at least rationally permissible and arguably rationally obligatory (13, 249).

The first part of the book consists of four chapters defending theism, the belief in one Creator God. In chapter 1, after briefly introducing the cosmological arguments of Thomas Aquinas and of Gottfried Leibniz, Moreland presents a strong defense of Craig's *kalam* argument, drawing on set theory, modern cosmology, and other considerations. According to this argument, the universe had a beginning, and this beginning is best explained by the existence of a Beginner who himself has no beginning (18–42).

Chapter 2 discusses arguments for God's existence from design. Here Moreland helpfully distinguishes seven different kinds of design as well as five different forms of design arguments. After responding to objections to design arguments from David Hume and other philosophers, Moreland defends the probability version of the argument with an extended discussion of the analogy of someone getting a perfect bridge hand (43–75).

Chapter 3 presents an argument from mind. Here Moreland advances Christian thinking about the mind–body problem and defends the existence of the soul, a subject to which he returned many times in the course of his career. "Mind appears to be a basic feature of the cosmos and its origin at the level of finite persons is best explained by postulating a fundamental Mind who gave finite minds being and design" (103).

Chapter 4 finishes Moreland's defense of theism with a discussion of morality and the meaning of life. After analyzing and responding to a range of philosophical positions on these issues, Moreland concludes with a brief defense of Pascal's wager (131–32).

If the book had ended at this point it would have been an impressive contribution to Christian apologetics. The next two chapters, however, engage biblical scholarship with equal aplomb in defense of the historical reliability of the New Testament (chap. 5) and the resurrection of Jesus (chap. 6). Then Moreland devotes chapter 7 to science and Christianity, anticipating themes he treated in greater depth two years later in his book *Christianity and the Nature of Science*. Moreland's considerable work over the years on the philosophy of science is perhaps his greatest contribution to Christian thought. He carefully explains and assesses different views of the nature of science, competing models for relating science and theology, and both biblical and scientific issues in the creation–evolution debate (185–223).

To this day, many evangelicals consider *Scaling the Secular City* one of the best introductions to Christian apologetics.

By Moreland

jpmoreland.com. Moreland's website.

Moreland, J. P. *Christianity and the Nature of Science*. Grand Rapids: Baker, 1989.

_____. *Finding Quiet: My Story of Overcoming Anxiety and the Practices that Brought Peace*. Grand Rapids: Zondervan, 2019. Moreland suffered two major breakdowns due to a long-standing anxiety disorder and shares how he learned that scientific and spiritual resources can work together to overcome anxiety.

_____. *Love Your God with All Your Mind: The Role of Reason in the Life of the Soul.* Rev. and updated. Colorado Springs: NavPress, 2012. Important book calling on Christians to make the cultivation of reason part of their discipleship.

_____. *Scaling the Secular City: A Defense of Christianity.* Grand Rapids: Baker, 1987.

_____, and Kai Nielsen. *Does God Exist? The Great Debate.* Nashville: Thomas Nelson, 1993. Debate between Moreland and an atheist philosopher; includes analyses by and discussions with other atheist and Christian philosophers.

About Moreland

Gould, Paul M., and Richard Brian Davis, eds. *Loving God with Your Mind: Essays in Honor of J. P. Moreland.* Chicago: Moody, 2014. Essays exploring topics of importance in Moreland's teaching; includes a chronology and list of his writings.

28

PHILLIP E. JOHNSON
Darwin on Trial (1991)

> I approach the creation-evolution dispute not as a scientist but
> as a professor of law, which means among other things that I
> know something about the ways that words are used in argu-
> ments. What first drew my attention to the question was the
> way the rules of argument seemed to be structured to make it
> impossible to question whether what we are being told about
> evolution is really true. —Phillip E. Johnson, *Darwin on Trial*, 8.

Phillip E. Johnson (1940–) studied literature at Harvard
and law at the University of Chicago, clerked for Supreme
Court Justice Earl Warren, and was law professor at UC
Berkeley from 1967 to 2000. One could not ask for a more
respectable liberal pedigree. Yet Wikipedia describes Johnson as "co-founder of the pseudo-scientific intelligent design movement." The scientific impetus for the movement
came before Johnson in two landmark books by creden-
tialed scientists: *The Mystery of Life's Origin: Reassessing
Current Theories*, by Charles Thaxton, Walter Bradley, and
Roger Olsen (1984), and *Evolution: A Theory in Crisis*, by
Michael Denton (1985). What launched the "ID movement," however, was Johnson's *Darwin on Trial* (1991).

Johnson's first chapter sounded a number of themes
that crop up repeatedly in the book. The first was the lack

of clarity in the creation—evolution debate. Johnson distinguished between creation and "creation-science," the young-earth form of creationism advocated by fundamentalist Christians (4). Likewise, Johnson pointed out that advocates of naturalistic evolution often equivocate in their use of the term evolution. "'Evolution' can mean anything from the uncontroversial statement that bacteria 'evolve' resistance to antibiotics to the grand metaphysical claim that the universe and mankind 'evolved' entirely by purposeless, mechanical forces" (9).

The second major theme of Johnson's book was that evolutionists commonly presuppose that only a purely naturalistic account of origins can count as "science." Johnson quoted the National Academy of Sciences statement that "the most basic characteristic of science" is "reliance upon naturalistic explanations" (7). As Johnson explained, this presupposition guarantees the outcome regardless of the evidence.

Throughout *Darwin on Trial*, Johnson engaged not only Darwin but also two of evolution's most celebrated modern defenders, Richard Dawkins and Stephen Jay Gould. He began by examining the two concepts basic to the modern neo-Darwinian synthesis: natural selection and mutation (chaps. 2–3). After discussing how the fossil record has proved to be a problem for evolutionary theory (chap. 4), Johnson showed that evolutionists' claim that evolution is a "fact" turns on the sort of equivocation noted earlier (chap. 5). He then returned to the fossil record, focusing on claimed examples of transitional forms (chap.

6). After considering the question of molecular evidence for evolution and the problem of the origin of life (chaps. 7–8), Johnson targeted the heart of the philosophical problem: the rules of science (chap. 9). Here Johnson engaged Judge William Overton's decision in the 1981 case *McLean v. Arkansas Board of Education*. Johnson argued that Overton was misled by the equivocation problem and missed the question-begging assumption that only a purely naturalistic view can be entertained in science. Johnson concluded by arguing that Darwinists advocate religious claims (chap. 10), advance evolution as a dogma in education (ch. 11), and promote a form of pseudoscience since they claim evolution to be nonfalsifiable (chap. 12).

Although not strictly speaking a work of Christian apologetics, *Darwin on Trial* was a game-changer in how many apologists address issues of science and origins.

By Johnson

Johnson, Phillip E. *Darwin on Trial*. Washington, DC: Regnery Gateway, 1991. 20th anniversary edition, with an introduction by Michael Behe. Downers Grove, IL: IVP Books, 2010.

_____. "Darwinism on Trial." Public lecture at University of California Irvine. Posted on YouTube, July 10, 2014.

_____, and Denis O. Lamoureux. *Darwinism Defeated? The Johnson–Lamoureux Debate on Biological Origins*. Vancouver: Regent College Publishing, 1999. Interesting debate; includes responses by several other noted evolutionists and intelligent design theorists.

About Johnson

Dembski, William A., ed. *Darwin's Nemesis: Phillip Johnson and the Intelligent Design Movement.* Downers Grove, IL: Inter-Varsity Press, 2006.

www.darwinontrial.com. Website devoted to Johnson's life and writings, with links to his articles, reviews of his books, and audio and video files of his interviews and lectures.

29

RICHARD SWINBURNE
Is There a God? (1996)

The very same criteria which scientists use to reach their own theories lead us to move beyond those theories to a creator God who sustains everything in existence. —Richard Swinburne, *Is There a God*, 2.

Richard Swinburne (1934–) is a British philosopher who first specialized in philosophy of science but then shifted to philosophy of religion. While teaching at the University of Keele, Swinburne published a trilogy of books in defense of theism: *The Coherence of Theism*, *The Existence of God*, and *Faith and Reason*. He then became professor of philosophy at Oxford in 1985, retiring in 2002. At Oxford, Swinburne published a four-book series defending specifically Christian doctrines: *Responsibility and Atonement*, *Revelation*, *The Christian God*, and *Providence and the Problem of Evil*. In addition, he published books on miracles, the Resurrection, and the deity of Christ. In 1995, Swinburne converted from the Anglican Church to the Orthodox Church.

Swinburne's *Is There a God?* presented the argument of his theism trilogy for a more general readership. His own summary is worth quoting in full:

Scientists, historians, and detectives observe data and proceed thence to some theory about what best explains the occurrence of these data. We can analyse the criteria which they use in reaching a conclusion that a certain theory is better supported by the data than a different theory—that is, more likely, on the basis of those data, to be true. Using those same criteria, we find that the view that there is a God explains everything we observe, not just some narrow range of data. It explains the fact that there is a universe at all, that scientific laws operate within it, that it contains conscious animals and humans with very complex intricately organized bodies, that we have abundant opportunities for developing ourselves and the world, as well as the more particular data that humans report miracles and have religious experiences. In so far as scientific causes and laws explain some of these things (and in part they do), these very causes and laws need explaining, and God's action explains them. The very same criteria which scientists use to reach their own theories lead us to move beyond those theories to a creator God who sustains everything in existence (2).

Although Swinburne defended a form of theism, he rejected aspects of classical theism that he found incoherent. Most significantly, he argued that God knows only what it is logically possible to know, and hence that God does not know all future events that depend on creatures' free decisions. Likewise, he maintained that God is everlasting but not a "timeless" being.

Swinburne examined apparent evidence for and against God's existence and concluded that theism is significantly more probable than not. He admitted that it is always possible to challenge this or that element of his or any other theist's argument. He pointed out, though, that this is also true in science and other fields. "But life is short and we have to act on the basis of what such evidence as we have had time to investigate shows on balance to be probably true" (140).

By Swinburne

"Richard Swinburne." Center for Christian Thought. A series of video interviews with Swinburne on such subjects as the soul, arguments for God's existence, the new atheists, the atonement, and God as a necessary being.

Swinburne, Richard. *The Christian God*. Oxford: Clarendon, 1994.

_____. *The Coherence of Theism*. Clarendon Library of Logic and Philosophy. Oxford: Clarendon, 1977, 2016.

_____. *The Existence of God*. Oxford: Clarendon, 1979, 2004. Lays a careful methodological foundation before arguing on the basis of various considerations that "the balance of probability" is on the side of theism.

_____. *Faith and Reason*. Oxford: Clarendon, 1981, 2005. Academic study (for advanced students) setting forth Swinburne's probabilistic approach to religious knowledge.

_____. *Is There a God?* Oxford: Oxford University Press, 1996, 2010. Less technical, and therefore less intimidating, presentation of Swinburne's sophisticated defense of belief in God.

_____ *Providence and the Problem of Evil*. Oxford: Clarendon, 1998.

_____. *Responsibility and Atonement*. Oxford: Clarendon, 1989.

_____. *Revelation: From Metaphor to Analogy*. Oxford: Clarendon, 1992, 2007.

_____. *The Resurrection of God Incarnate*. Oxford: Oxford University Press, 2003.

_____. *Was Jesus God?* Oxford: Oxford University Press, 2010.

About Swinburne

Bergmann, Michael, and Jeffrey E. Brower, eds. *Reason & Faith: Themes from Richard Swinburne*. Oxford: Oxford University Press, 2016. Essays by philosophers on such topics as divine simplicity, defining omnipotence, Swinburne's view of atonement, and so on.

Gotobed, Julian. "Richard Swinburne." Boston Collaborative Encyclopedia of Western Theology. Online encyclopedia entry giving a detailed introduction to Swinburne. Online at http://people.bu.edu/wwildman/bce/swinburne.htm.

Padgett, Alan G., ed. *Reason and the Christian Religion: Essays in Honour of Richard Swinburne*. Oxford: Clarendon; New York: Oxford University Press, 1994. Includes Swinburne's "Intellectual Autobiography" (1–18).

30

LEE STROBEL

The Case for Christ (1998)

> As far as I was concerned, the case was closed. There was enough proof for me to rest easy with the conclusion that the divinity of Jesus was nothing more than the fanciful invention of superstitious people. Or so I thought. —Lee Strobel, *The Case for Christ*, 15.

Lee Strobel (1952–) was an award-winning journalist and legal editor for the *Chicago Tribune* who earned recognition for his coverage of the Ford Pinto trial, which was also the subject of his first book (1980). At the time, he was an atheist. When his wife started attending church, Strobel applied his journalistic methods to determine whether Christianity was true, eventually concluding that it was. Strobel's story is presented in his best-selling book *The Case for Christ: A Journalist's Personal Investigation of the Evidence for Jesus*, which features interviews with 13 Christian scholars. He went on to publish a series of these "Case" books, including some children's versions, and in 2017 a theatrical film based on his conversion story was released.

Each chapter of *The Case for Christ* opened with a legal case from Strobel's time as a journalist, including the Ford Pinto case at the beginning of chapter 3. These "case files" illustrated the types of issues discussed in the chapters, such as eyewitnesses, documents, scientific data, and the like. In the rest of each chapter, Strobel gave a first-person account of his interview with a Christian scholar with expertise in the subject at hand. While these particular interviews were conducted years after he had become a Christian, he did ask them some hard questions similar to those an atheist might pose.

Strobel's lineup of expert witnesses for his "case" was stellar. He began with Craig Blomberg answering questions about whether the Gospels are based on reliable, eyewitness testimonies. Bruce Metzger was the expert called to testify regarding the textual preservation of the Gospels. Strobel's experts on the empty tomb, the resurrection appearances of Jesus, and circumstantial evidence confirming the Resurrection were William Lane Craig, Gary Habermas, and J. P. Moreland. Even the lesser-known experts turn out to be informative and fascinating. For example, in Strobel's interview with Louis Lapide on whether Jesus was the Messiah, Lapide gave his own testimony as a Jew who was surprised to find that the New Testament was not the anti-Semitic handbook he had expected.

The book concluded with Strobel's brief review of the evidence and his personal testimony of becoming a Christian. He admitted that when he was an atheist he had lived "a profane, drunken, self-absorbed, and immoral lifestyle," stabbing colleagues in the back to get ahead (268). A few months after turning to Christ for forgiveness and salvation, his life had changed so much for the better than even his five-year-old daughter noticed the difference (269–70).

It is fitting that our overview of the history of Christian apologetics through the end of the twentieth century concludes with Strobel's book. We began with Luke's two-volume history of the origins of the Christian faith, written at least in part as a defense of Paul, and noted Luke's emphasis on the use of eyewitness testimonies (Luke 1.1–4). With Strobel's defense of Christianity consisting of interviews of scholarly "witnesses" on the historical reliability of the Gospels' accounts, we have come full circle.

By Strobel

https://leestrobel.com. Strobel's website.

Strobel, Lee. *The Case for Christ: A Journalist's Personal Investigation of the Evidence for Jesus*. Grand Rapids: Zondervan, 1998.

_____. *The Case for a Creator: A Journalist Investigates Evidence that Points toward God*. Grand Rapids: Zondervan, 2004.

_____. *The Case for Faith: A Journalist Investigates the Toughest Objections to Christianity*. Grand Rapids: Zondervan, 2000.

_____. *The Case for Miracles: A Journalist Investigates Evidence for the Supernatural*. Grand Rapids: Zondervan, 2018.

_____. *The Case for the Real Jesus: A Journalist Investigates Current Attacks on the Identity of Christ*. Grand Rapids: Zondervan, 2007.

About Strobel

The Case for Christ. DVD, 2017. Theatrical film based on Strobel's conversion story.

FURTHER RESOURCES

Boa, Kenneth D., and Robert M. Bowman Jr. *Faith Has Its Reasons: Integrative Approaches to Defending the Christian Faith.* 2nd ed. Downers Grove, IL: InterVarsity Press—Biblica Books, 2006. A comprehensive textbook surveying all of the major contemporary approaches to apologetics, categorized broadly as classical apologetics, evidentialism, Reformed apologetics (which includes presuppositionalism and Reformed Epistemology), and fideism. In this book, Kenneth Boa and I encouraged Christian apologists to integrate strong elements from other approaches into their preferred approach. Presents significant treatments of the apologetic thought of more than 50 Christian thinkers in relation to their varying apologetic methods, including all but four of the thinkers discussed in this book.

Bush, L. Russ, ed. *Classical Readings in Christian Apologetics, A.D. 100–1800.* Grand Rapids: Zondervan—Academie, 1983. Excellent short collection of readings from Justin Martyr, Origen, Augustine, Anselm, Aquinas, Calvin, Butler, Paley, and four other apologists.

Campbell-Jack, W. C., and Gavin McGrath, eds. *New Dictionary of Christian Apologetics.* C. Stephen Evans, consulting ed. Leicester, England, and Downers Grove, IL: InterVarsity, 2006. International reference work with articles by numerous contributing scholars, covering a wide range of topics and thinkers.

Edgar, William, and K. Scott Oliphint, eds. *Christian Apologetics Past & Present: A Primary Source Reader.* 2 vols. Wheaton, IL: Crossway Books, 2009, 2011. Volume 1 covers up to 1500 and includes readings from the New Testament, Justin Martyr, Origen, Augustine (with about a hundred pages for him alone), Anselm, Aquinas, and ten other authors. Volume 2 covers authors since 1500 including Calvin (with about 70 pages), Pascal, Butler, Paley, Kierkegaard, Orr, Van Til, C. S. Lewis, Schaeffer, Plantinga, Craig, and 15 other authors.

Evans, C. Stephen. *Pocket Dictionary of Apologetics and Philosophy of Religion.* Downers Grove, IL: InterVarsity Press, 2002. Useful reference with brief definitions and explanations of key terms and descriptions of the views of various thinkers.

House, H. Wayne, and Dennis W. Jowers. *Reasons for Our Hope: An Introduction to Christian Apologetics.* Nashville: B&H, 2011. Textbook includes about a hundred pages on the history of apologetics, introducing many of the figures discussed in this book.

Samples, Kenneth Richard. *Classic Christian Thinkers: An Introduction.* Covina, CA: RTB Press, 2019. Introductions to nine great Christian thinkers from the second to the twentieth centuries, including six of the ones discussed here (Augustine, Anselm, Aquinas, Calvin, Pascal, and C. S. Lewis). Each chapter includes a helpful summary of what we can learn from that thinker today. An excellent place to go if you want to learn more about these authors.

Sweis, Khaldoun A., and Chad V. Meister, eds. *Christian Apologetics: An Anthology of Primary Sources.* Grand Rapids: Zondervan, 2012. This textbook presents 54 thematically arranged readings from authors throughout church history.

The authors presented include Augustine, Anselm, Aquinas (four readings, the most for any author), Calvin, Pascal, Paley, Lewis, Schaeffer, Geisler, Montgomery, Craig, Moreland, Swinburne, and many more.

ABOUT FAITH THINKERS

Faith Thinkers is an nonprofit, evangelical Christian apologetics ministry helping Christians to think more deeply and express themselves more clearly about what they believe and why they believe it. We direct believers to resources, mostly those produced by other apologists, from which they can find answers to their faith questions and become better equipped to share the truth of Christianity with others. Our aim is to help you love God with all your mind and love your neighbor as yourself by speaking the truth to them in love. To that end, we encourage you to learn from a wide range of good Christian thinkers (as exemplified in this book) and to develop your own mature, well-informed Christian mind. We also provide research and editorial support for other Christians writing in apologetics. You can find us online at **www.FaithThinkers.org**.

FAITH THINKERS

For a full listing of our books, visit DeWard's website:

www.deward.com

DeWard™

for your journey